PLAN B
RUN BABY RUN

Printed in the United States of America

Tamarind Press, LLC
1209 Mountain Road Place NE, Suite 6654
Albuquerque, NM 87110

Description: Learn about modern threats to privacy and strategies to counter
them. Asset protection and anonymity.

Keywords: Plan B; Privacy; Vanishing Acts; How to Disappear;
How To Be Invisible

Library of Congress Cataloging-in-Publication Data is available on file.

ISBN: 979-8-218-72010-0 (Paperback)

NOTICE TO READERS

PLAN B

Run Baby Run

GD APPLEGATE

Tamarind Press, LLC

TABLE OF CONTENTS

INTRODUCTION

First off, this book is not written to help readers break the law, evade taxes, or engage in otherwise illegal or morally reprehensible behavior. It is primarily a work of fiction but also meant to offer some ideas on how to make your private life more *private*. And if you really, *really* had to run, then we can offer suggestions as to how you could do it and what things would look like in a post-vanishing act. Of course, it's all a fantasy meant for entertainment. That is true particularly of Chapter One, which takes the reader through the predicament of imaginary characters in need of disappearing. So feel free to enjoy those stories with a glass of your favorite drink. But if the opposition is already knocking on your door, make sure to skip to Chapter Two before it's too late!

Over the years, fascinating books have been written about techniques on how to disappear. Most of them, however, are dated, in the sense that they were written before critical technological advances, which are employed by both governments and private companies, came on the scene. Furthermore, the explosion of online activities and social media has demolished most of ordinary people's privacy, to the advantage of commercial marketers and advertisers. Worse yet, there is a growing acceptance by the overwhelming majority of the public that a loss of privacy is an inevitable part of progress.

Recent writers have focused on the technical aspects of protecting privacy, and we have a lot to learn from them. But from a practical point of view, we find that a nexus is missing between a defense of privacy and the arduous task of going anonymous or disappearing.

This book is not meant to be a study or compilation of materials. It was mostly born out of reflection and with personal experience and knowledge as its only guides. Informal interviews that do not require quotes were a secondary source, along with open source and general information. For those reasons, you will not see footnotes but only plain text. If you do not like what you read, feel free to blame the author directly as the sole bearer of responsibility for the book's content.

What we are offering here is a general discussion of privacy and techniques to withdraw from the information web surrounding us. But the book is still a work of fiction and fantasy with no connection to real persons or places. We are not passing judgment on those who wish to withdraw from their ordinary life or on their motives, nor are we endorsing any activities that run counter to the laws of any particular place.

Some people seek a more private lifestyle, while others are actually trying to disappear altogether. In both scenarios, they will be faced with forces opposing their efforts, and those forces may in fact be the reason why they are trying to flee in the first place. Generally speaking, one can imagine various challenges in the quest for freedom. They can include jealous spouses, nosy relatives or friends, private investigators, skip tracers, government agencies, and foreign governments. Sometimes there can be a combination of these. For the sake of simplicity, throughout this book all forces that constitute an obstacle to someone's efforts to go private or disappear will be referred to as "the opposition."

Sometimes, the destination or intended destination of someone who wishes to disappear is referred to in this book as "The Land of the Disappeared." Of course, there is no such place but, once again, we are trying to simplify concepts and language. The word "run" in the title does not imply or recommend a strategy for surrender. On the contrary, running refers to a course of action to safeguard one's life or privacy. Perhaps to make a later comeback and strike at the opposition like never before.

We take no position on the debate on gender identity and pronouns. For the sake of simplicity, however, when the pronouns "he" or "she" can be used interchangeably, we have used the feminine "she." Likewise, when "his" or "her" can be used interchangeably, we have used "her."

ONE

IT COULD HAPPEN TO YOU

A Night To Remember

It's almost midnight on a chilly autumn night. You are sitting on a comfortable chair next to the fireplace in your old cabin near Swan Lake. You are in the living room, located on the first floor. It is such a pleasure to relax with a classic book (in print no less) and a glass of wine or two after a long and stressful day. A steady drizzle beats on the windows and accompanies the song of the wind chimes outside. You are alone but not lonely. So much to think about and so many dreams still unrealized. If it weren't for the engrossing story in the book, this would be an ideal opportunity for reflection. Some downtime to go over past events in your life and the decisions you have made. A time to chase away, once and for all, those crazy thoughts that pop up in your mind every so often, like demons that can't find peace. The unreasonable belief that maybe things could be different, if only you had the guts to jump–to break away from an ordinary life that no longer fulfills. But the book really grabs you, and there is really no time for anything else right now.

You are starting to get sleepy when a noise outside the house, near the main door, catches your attention. You put it down to the wind, or a fallen branch. The yard needs so much work this time of year, and there is always something more important to do. You take another sip of wine and go back to the book. But a few minutes later, a loud crash in the foyer leaves no doubt: An intruder has just broken in. You can't see the action but can hear the glass falling from the broken window and heavy steps. In an instinctive reaction, you jump up and run to the opposite side of the room, open an old chest, and grab a gun from inside. It is a legally owned and registered gun that you keep just for the unlikely event that you might need to defend yourself–for a rainy day, if you will. And it's raining now: It's pouring!

You head toward the foyer to confront the intruder, but before you can even reach the door, he appears in the living room–fit looking and big, with wild hair and bizarre clothes. He seems to be holding something, a dark object almost a foot in length, maybe a gun. But you do not even try to guess his intentions. You only have time for one survival decision: It's him or you! And you decide it's going to be you. As you walk back and turn, you straighten the arm holding the gun and bring the left hand under the right wrist and grab it. Before the intruder even has a chance to move, you aim and fire two shots in quick succession–one to the heart and one to the head. He drops to the floor while you walk back in shock.

In the blink of an eye, your life has changed. Everything you have known and taken for granted is gone–just like a car accident or a heart attack. One minute everything is right and normal, and the next it's all over. You drop the gun and bring your hands up to cover your face as if to cry. You are confused, horrified, and frightened. You sit back in your chair, look at the fire, and breathe deeply. Your heart is racing as you try to plan the next move.

As you try and assess the situation, your first thought is to call the police. You are about to get up and look for your mobile, but then you start having second thoughts. What happens if you call the police and report the incident? You killed an intruder in self-defense. But, wait a minute, is he really dead? You get up and walk over to the still body. You take the pulse and, sure enough, there is no pulse–dead as a door nail! And there is a gun on the floor, but it does not appear to be a working and loaded gun. You go back to the chair and sit. Close your eyes and think. Think of what to say to the police.

In the first few minutes after the traumatic event, you have been making an assumption. You have been thinking that you have acted in self-defense and that that is the truth and is what you are going to tell the police–an open-and-shut case. No need to lie. But what is self-defense? You are not a lawyer, but you are starting to think that maybe there are limits to self-defense. Of course, an intruder in your house that *appears* to be carrying a gun is a big enough threat to take action. But what action is appropriate and commensurate to counter the threat? Could you have disarmed the man? Warned him? As it turns out, you never tried to warn, disarm, or even run from the room. You did not even limit yourself to stop the man's actions. You aimed straight for the heart, with a .357 Magnum and fired. And then fired another shot to the head, execution-style.

The more you think about it, the more you worry that the case is not going to be so easy or straightforward. There is a chance, if only a chance, that you will be charged with a crime. And if that happened, you would need to hire a defense lawyer. Surely, you could get someone to take your testimony, clarify the facts, and close the case. But, from the little you know about these cases, and your experience is limited to television shows and newspaper articles, it can get complicated. If the prosecutor decides to take the case, they will press for a conviction, or at least some form of plea. Even the legal work leading up to a plea would require a significant amount of your lawyer's time and attorney's fees. And if the case went to trial, the attorney's fees would go through the roof. You have heard that some indigent defendants get a public defender. But you are employed and may not qualify for government aid. And how good are these public defenders anyway? No, you would have to retain a private lawyer that will cost you a fortune. You may lose your house and every cent you have ever put away. All this money and aggravation may help you get acquitted, but what if you lost the case? What if you ended up in jail? You have heard what happens to some inmates, and just the thought of it sends a chill through your spine.

If you were lucky, the police would not charge you. And that would be the end of that. Or would it? Unfortunately for you, the reality of these cases is that the threshold for a criminal conviction or even indictment is a lot higher than it is for bringing a civil action. Even though a prosecutor may decline to indict because she feels that the evidence is insufficient to obtain a conviction, a private party might choose to take a chance on a civil lawsuit. The family of the intruder would probably try to recover all of the money they could get from you. They could sue for things like wrongful death, violation of civil rights, and many other plaintiff theories. You would then need to hire a civil defense lawyer, a litigator. But defending a civil lawsuit of this kind would cost a huge amount of money, even if you win. And you might lose because of the manner in which you handled your self-defense. The plaintiffs could claim that your victim was just a homeless person looking for food. Or that he was mentally unstable and vulnerable. That he was looking for shelter on a dark, rainy night. They might be able to show that his gun was not even loaded and was inoperable. That he would not have been able to hurt you even if he had wanted to. That you are a fit young man, whereas your victim had health issues that made him incapable of hurting an armed person like you. They could claim that you deliberately killed your victim, execution-style, without any hesitation.

The more you think about your predicament, the more your situation appears hopeless. Realistically, there is no way you can get out of this problem without losing everything you have, everything you've ever worked for. You will end up with a judgment that will wipe out not only your current assets, but also all of your future assets, along with a portion of all of your future earnings and your pension. If, for the sake of argument, you are so lucky that the government does not prosecute and family members of your victim choose not to sue (they have several years to decide), your problems may not be over.

Unfortunately, there can be other aspects of a situation like this that can make legal problems look insignificant by comparison. A possible challenge could be the reaction of family and friends or accomplices of the intruder you just shot. The way you look at the events, you understand, is subjective. To your way of thinking, you defended yourself from an armed intruder who may have been on the point of killing you. You own the house where you live. You worked for it, for God's sake. You have a right to be there. You have a right to your security and your privacy. What right does a stranger have to crash into your home and ruin your life? This is the way you think because you hold certain values that you have learned from your parents, the schools you attended, and your community. Your social class, if you will. But those values are by no means universal. Someone who has grown up in a different community or has lived in underprivileged circumstances may view life, and the incident, in a different light. They might question the very nature of private property. In their view, someone may own something that, in all fairness, should belong to them. And it is only circumstances that determine who gets to sit as lord of the manor and who gets left on the outside looking in–on a rainy night.

Your victim, the one you killed in execution-style, may have been someone's father, brother, husband, lover, or friend. He may have been someone's childhood friend, maybe someone's hero. Who knows how many good deeds he may have done? He may leave a trail of sorrow behind or a family to support. Any of the relatives or friends of the victim may feel that a loved one has been taken away from them. They may believe that someone like you, so different from them and so evil, has taken one of their own, by acting as judge, jury, and executioner. Even though the government might not prosecute you, and especially if they do not prosecute you, in the eyes of your victim's loved ones, you are guilty. You are guilty of a terrible crime for which you need to pay. And even if you are prosecuted, the outcome might not satisfy the victim's loved ones. The court system, they may feel, is stacked against them: a system designed to protect the privilege that has been accorded to some, and denied to others.

Revenge is a dish that is best served cold. It is not worth much if it is inflicted in the heat of passion or as a sudden reaction to an event. The best part of revenge in fact is the infliction of psychological pain: the pain that comes from anxiety, fear, and uncertainty; the uncertainty of the future, caused by the fear that something bad, very bad, is going to happen. And this state in which you find yourself now is going to be the new normal.

Your victim's loved ones are going to go after you, and you can be sure of that. They, of course, know where you live. They know your name and what you look like. They can easily find out your schedule and your habits. They can see which car you drive and who visits you and when. From the lights in your house, they can see which rooms you occupy and when. Conversely, you know nothing about them. You don't know who is going to go after you or when. And you do not know what they are planning to do. They could start a fire while you sleep. They could shoot you through a window or when you walk out of the house, or follow you when you drive away. And the toughest part of it all is that whatever is coming may happen tomorrow, next week, or a year from now. Meanwhile, you will be living in fear and without hope because in reality no one is really going to help you. The police will not help you based on your fear that someone might exact revenge against you, especially since you don't even know who that person or persons might be. A dog would be of very limited use since it could be poisoned or shot. Private security would be out of the question as you would need three teams to take turns to cover you around the clock.

No, you are not going to call the police after all. But what can you do? If you run away, they will eventually find the body and charge you with murder. You will end up on a most wanted list. And that would also mean abandoning the property and most of your possessions. You could move, and maybe you should move, but you need to dispose of the body in some way. Have you tried disposing of a body lately? That is a mighty task indeed (see the chapter on forensics). As you sit in your chair, drenched in sweat and with a dry mouth, you are looking at the body of a 200-pound man. You are no expert on this, but you can easily figure out that carrying the body would be very difficult. And where would you carry it to? Not the lake, as it would eventually be found even if you weighted it down. Cutting it up would be a most distasteful job for which you would need several tools and heavy plastic bags. But the main problem would be the DNA spreading all over the room. And the relatives and friends or accomplices of the departed, now cut in various parts and removed from the house, may figure out the last place he visited. The broken window, which may take a while to get fixed, would be a telltale sign of the intrusion. At the very least, you could expect "inquiries" from the loved ones of the intruder or from the police.

With the gravity of the situation becoming apparent, you start to go back to the thoughts about your life–your accomplishments, your disappointments, and your frustrations. You begin to wonder if a way out exists, not only from your current predicament, but also from your life in general. You start considering a new life somewhere else, maybe with a new identity. You start exploring the types of work you could do if you could get a new beginning. But can you really get away from it all? Maybe you can or could if you had a Plan B and read this book!

Damsel in Distress

You are a woman in your late twenties. You have a nice job and live in a small apartment with your two cats. You are in good health, and everything seems to be going well in your life. Your boyfriend is the envy of your girlfriends–tall, dark, and handsome, with enough of a mystery aura about him to make things interesting and so passionate!

You lead what could be considered an ordinary life. Lately, however, there is something about your boyfriend that is not quite right. The way he looks at you with those crazy eyes of his is strange. He is not as talkative as he used to be. But the biggest surprise comes when you discover parts of his missing dog in the freezer. In addition to that, some leftovers you saw in the trash lead you to believe that he has been eating the dog. And now he is coming after you. He starts with an eerie laugh and swears he is going to murder you. He makes strange sounds and faces and then breaks out again in his strange laughter. This new behavior is shocking, and you talk about it with your friends and your mother. The consensus is that you should go to the police. So, at the earliest opportunity, you visit the police station in your neighborhood.

It takes you some time before you are able to have an interview with an officer. But even more frustrating is her unwillingness to cooperate and help you. The police mean well, you are sure. But there are some technical issues with your report that cannot be overcome. Your story is all true: Namely, you are dating someone that is displaying strange and very troubling behavior. He has your address and knows where you work. He knows the car you drive. He has stated several times that he intends to kill you. He is a strong man and, you happen to know, has a gun hobby. All that makes you an easy target and should enable you to get some kind of police protection or a stay-away order from the court. Unfortunately, it does not work that way.

For one thing, even in a small town, the police have more pressing matters than getting involved in lovers' quarrels. Your story may be true, but the police cannot confirm it unless they get a warrant to inspect the freezer with the remains of the dog. And, more important, there is no evidence that a crime has been committed. Even if what you saw, or think you saw, are the remains of a dog, how do you, or the police, know that it was really the missing dog? And even if it is, the most serious thing your boyfriend could be charged with is cruelty to animals. But it would need to be proven that he deliberately killed the dog, which may or may not be an offense. And the dog could have died of natural causes. Or your boyfriend could have found it dead somewhere. The police are not going to offer protection over unsubstantiated charges without evidence of a crime having been committed.

You soon let your boyfriend know that you are ending the relationship. You mention irreconcilable differences, your need to be alone for a while, your not being ready for a serious relationship. But, of course, he is not buying any of it. He is enraged and promises to kill you, *and* to eat you! At this point, you know that he is going to get you, so you go back to the police and update them on the latest developments. But the reaction is the same. Only this time, they suggest you could go to a battered women unit in the clerk's office of the county family court. There you could file paperwork for a stay-away court order. You immediately go there but run into a brick wall. The court would need corroborating evidence of your story even before they set a hearing. Since a crime has not been committed, or at least not *yet*, there are no grounds on which to issue any kind of restraining order. The fact that you find your boyfriend's behavior strange and that you *claim* he has threatened you is just not enough.

The main problem you are facing, however, is the following. Even assuming that you could get a stay-away or restraining order against your boyfriend, what good would it do? If he is not concerned about the consequences of committing murder, is he going to worry about violating an order from a county judge? Obviously not, which leaves you in clear danger of becoming the victim of a madman. You could move, but where to? Your boyfriend knows the car you drive, your job location, your mother's address, and he has met most of your girlfriends. He would be able to track you down very quickly. Unless…Unless you had a Plan B–a place to go and something to do beyond the reach of your boyfriend.

Election Night

You live in a large, powerful country where they just had important elections, but you haven't been paying much attention. Between the hard work schedule, sports, social activities, dating, travel, and many other things, there just isn't much time left for reading up on politics. And besides, in a wealthy, democratic nation, things are going to be just fine, or are they?

It's not easy getting up after a bad night's sleep. It's already past nine o'clock. Obviously, the damn alarm app didn't work. It either sounds multiple times or not at all, like today. You head for the kitchen to make some coffee. Maybe that will take care of the hangover from last night's parties. What is it about alcohol, indigestion, and night-mares? Which comes first? Do bad dreams reflect a general anxiety about things we fear, or are they a premonition of bad things about to happen? You look at your phone, and you can see that something strange is going on–lots of texts, emails, and WhatsApp messages! But you are not ready yet for the busy day ahead, so you go back to your coffee and some cookies from a cool new store, and then return to the phone to read the news. Election results are in, and they jump at you. Boy, oh boy, just a few days ago, the clock went back 1 hour for the end of daylight savings time! You thought that it wasn't going to change until Spring, but now it looks like it's gone back another 100 years! So that's what the messages were about.

You call a few friends and a colleague, and then go back to the news. It looks like there're lots of unhappy people around–really unhappy! So much so that some are planning to head for the hills and leave the country. They already have articles and websites on how to emigrate–lots of information! It all sounds interesting and scary at the same time. You may be tempted to run–a clean break from the routine and a new beginning somewhere else, another roll of the dice. But what about your job, career, family, friends, commitments, debts, and other entanglements? Not to mention some legal issues you are facing that make travel tempting but problematic. "Possession of cocaine with intent to distribute" is a serious charge, and your trial is coming up. Would vanishing look good in the eyes of the law? And what about Fiona? Did she say she wants to get pregnant, or is she pregnant already? You just can't remember exactly.

The trouble with your relationship with Fiona is that she may not appreciate your vanishing act if you decided to "jump." And that could have a major impact on your legal case because she was present during the incident that led to your arrest. She was in the car at the time of the stop. She has not been charged yet, but that could change, and your lawyer heard from the prosecutor that charges are pending–complicated stuff but a real messy situation! So much so that your lawyer keeps talking about adversarial interests that prevent him from representing both you and Fiona. What happens at your trial may well hinge on her testimony. Because if she becomes estranged after your vanishing act, she will be sure to retain her own defense counsel. And that lawyer may well advise her to "sell you down the river," especially if you're gone.

But one thing is for sure: If you take a plea or go down at trial, you will be required to surrender your passport even before sentencing and appeal. And speaking of passports, yours is about to expire, so you will need to renew it, and time is short.

As you sip on your coffee while you nurse your hangover, you reflect on your situation. The more you think about it, the worse it looks. In general, life is not so bad, but there are complications. You are in legal jeopardy. You are or may soon be pressured into parental responsibilities you want nothing to do with. You owe a considerable amount of money. And now you are sure that the country is going to shit. So the idea of heading to the Land of the Disappeared looks more appealing than ever. But time is not on your side, now that you need to plan so much and to make hard decisions. Time that you don't have. If only you had planned for a rainy day when the sun was still shining. If only you had a Plan B in place. If only you had read this book!

Another Whistle Blower Bites the Dust

Imagine working for a large company for 20 years–a model employee throughout your career, rising from clerical work in your twenties to management. But, lately, you have come to discover a disturbing practice of the company that you had long suspected but never verified. Now you are sure: Your employer's operations are resulting in pollution of a nearby river and reservoir that provides drinking water to the local population. The clues are many. It started with reports of birth defects and rates of a certain type of cancer that are far above the norm. Then, there were people who claimed to have seen company employees actually dumping canisters of an unknown substance into the river. And then, by sheer chance, you ran into a memo that was sent by the vice president of the company to the PR director and the person in charge of security. The letter addressed reports of environmental problems and ways to deal with them. It suggested contacting those circulating derogatory information about the company with a carrot-and-stick approach. The company could offer them jobs or even cash if they kept quiet. And veiled threats could be made if they failed to cooperate. Mention could be made that the company had detailed information about the persons involved, including their address and those of their family members. In fact, the veiled threats could be the firing shot of the discussion, so that the person could clearly understand the benefits of cooperation.

The choices presented to you are few, and basically boil down to these: either keep quiet or risk losing your job and many of your colleague friends. Your niece and cousin also work for the company. You live in what they call a one-company town. You discuss the situation with your ex-husband and your brother. They are troubled by the news and are not sure how to advise you. After an agonizing inner struggle, you decide to go public with the information. But first you try to talk to the vice president whose name is on the memo, without mentioning the memo itself. You plan to say something like, "It has come to my attention that an effort is under way to…"

The VP's reaction is brutal. He denies any knowledge of the problem and even implies that you may be trying to extort money from the company by making threats. He has looked at your personnel file before he meets with you and brings up some financial problems you seem to be having. He threatens to fire you and your niece if you repeat to anyone your accusation of environmental violations. But you have made a copy of the memo and now plan to use it.

Your strategy is to go straight to a reporter for a small publication in the area. After making an appointment, you meet the reporter and go over the facts that you have uncovered but make no mention of the memo. As it turns out, withholding the memo is a good idea. Of course, the reporter knows the company and many people that work there. The news you bring is not welcome. He seems very uneasy. He then starts challenging your claims, using the usual tactics that are employed in these cases by those trying to cover up an uncomfortable truth. He casts doubt on eyewitnesses' accounts, disparages the doctors who have raised the possibility of water contamination (he knows the doctors personally), and generally dismisses the problem. But promises to think about it and investigate, as is his duty to do as a press reporter.

Not 2 days go by before you get an urgent call from the same company VP you approached in the beginning. They call you in for a meeting. The VP is there, along with two people from security, a secretary, a company lawyer from the counsel's office, and another person you don't know. Their message amounts to this: Stop your disruptive and defaming activity, or else! They warn you that there could be legal consequences to your actions and that your job, as well as your reputation, are on the line. The lawyer nods in approval while the secretary takes notes. You leave the VP's office in tears but determined to press on with your newfound crusade.

One option for you would be to go to the police and report the alleged environmental violations. But your instinct somehow tells you that that would not be a good idea for several reasons, not least of which is the fact that the local police know the company well, and a number of their friends and relatives work there. It could also be, but you do not know for sure, that some officers are on the payroll of the company.

Which could explain why there have never been any criminal complaints brought against employees of the company for repeated and brazen dumping of chemicals in local waters, even in daylight. Another possibility would be to go to a law firm and suggest a class action on behalf of residents who have been damaged by the alleged environmental violations. The problem with that is that a law firm in another city might not be interested in the case. And a local firm would most likely know lawyers from the counsel's office of the company. It is very unlikely that they would go against local colleagues. Your conclusion is that only a major newspaper would run the story if you could back it up.

You have not even begun to pursue your allegations with the press, but when you come home a few days later, you find firefighters and police patrol cars in front of your house. You are very alarmed, but it turns out that it was only an isolated fire in the toolshed. You have not been in the toolshed in months, so it is clear to you that it was arson. You are tempted to mention to the police the veiled threats you have received from the company you work for but think better of it. So that was clearly a message from the company, a sure sign of worse things to come. In a frenzy, you contact a security company and manage to have them install a security system. The windows are secured with almost-invisible wires running on the side of the glass. If there were a breach, an alarm would go off at the office of the security company, which in turn would alert the police. You then add a security lock to the main door, and the picket fence is replaced with a sturdy wire fence and gate. That type of fence is not a big obstacle for would-be intruders, but they would need wire cutters to gain access, as opposed to just walking into the yard from the street. That would be considered breaking and entering, which is a crime. As further discouragement to intruders, you get a guard dog and place a doghouse right behind the house. The dog can live there, at least during the warmer months.

After putting in place the new security measures, you feel a little better about your situation. And then start to focus again on your newfound mission of exposing a major polluter. Your first move is to research the newspapers and the reporters who are likely to be interested in the story. They are all in the big cities. After a number of phone calls, you secure an appointment with a journalist who works 3 hours away from you. You go and see him on a Saturday. You agree to meet at a diner on a nearby country road, well away from the office of the newspaper where he works. He listens to your story, reads the copy of the memo, and appears to be interested in the case. But he mentions that there is another reporter who may be better suited to investigate and break the story. A new meeting is going to be necessary.

When your started your research, on your home computer, and used your cell phone to call the various newspapers, you assumed that your communications were private. That was a wrong assumption, but then again, you had not read this book yet. By the time you get back home, it is almost seven in the evening. What you encounter is an eerie silence, and even as you open the gate and enter your property, there is no sign of the dog. The only noticeable thing is red paint splashed on your door. You hesitate to enter and choose instead to check the backyard and the doghouse. To your horror, you see the dog lying on his back, dead. There are no signs of blood or injuries to the dog, so you assume it has been poisoned. This time you call the police as you want to be on record with a complaint about harassment and damages to your property as well as animal cruelty. But of course, the complaint is against persons unknown, so it won't help you now.

The next thing you do is to go and buy one of those prepaid phones that you will learn more about in this book. You need to activate it, an operation that could probably link it back to you. But at least you are putting some distance between you and your tormentors. You are only going to use this phone for critical communications regarding your mission. And the first call is to your new journalist friend to explain your predicament and set a new appointment to meet the reporter who may be covering the case. The appointment is for the following Saturday, near the city where the original reporter works. But you meet at a different location, a nondescript coffee shop that caters to blue-collar workers in the area. The original reporter is there with the other journalist who may take over the story. He has been briefed already. You are introduced to each other and exchange some information. You describe in detail the latest attack on your property and the poisoning of the dog. The original reporter sits back and listens. The new guy is hooked. He wants to do a preliminary investigation and then run a series of stories describing the activities of the company and its alleged environmental violations. Of course, he is also going to interview company officials, if they agree to it.

The operation is on and so is the heat. But there is an agreement to hold off until you are ready to take a leave of absence from work and move to a safe location. You can do it easily because your ex-husband no longer lives with you, and the children are grown and gone. The issue of your security was discussed with the newspaper, and they gave you assurances that something could be done to protect you once "the boat started to rock." They mentioned some kind of whistleblower protection. They also mentioned a government program to render you anonymous and maybe relocate you. Which government agency, however, they did not mention.

You start packing your bags and give notice to the employer about needing to take some time off. Your plan is to go stay with an old aunt, a widow, who lives a few hours from you. Things seem to be settling down for now when, without warning to you, the first installment of the story runs. It is picked up by other news services and the local TV station. All this before you even move. You are starting to panic and fear the worst when, a day later, early in the morning, you hear a loud explosion. Somebody blew up your car. You call the newspaper reporter that you originally met. He does not seem to be in the loop anymore and refers you to the reporter handling the story. You reach him soon after, but he seems to be a bit aloof. You explain the latest events, but when you bring up the protection issues that you had discussed, he seems to be vague. He needs to consult with some colleagues. You call him back that evening, and he has no news. He suggests that you call the police.

At this point, you start looking at your situation more objectively. Your family is gone. In theory, you still have a job, but that is going to be gone soon. Your life is in danger. The police are unlikely to help you since you suspect that the attacks against your property came from the company but cannot prove it. For all intents and purposes, you are homeless since you can't safely live in your house any longer. There is a very good chance you will be sued by the company you helped expose. No lawyer is going to defend you from the onslaught of defamation actions likely to come from the company, unless you are able to pay a prodigious amount of money. But how are you going to do that without a job and a place to live? The local community, including colleagues, friends, and even some relatives are also going to be turning against you. So, the thought comes to you as a revelation. Can you get away, disappear, and be saved from all that is threatening you? Yes, you can. But you need a plan, a Plan B. If only you had one already, you would be in much better shape.

Oh, Freedom!

You are a man in your prime, so full of life and dreams– with so much you would like to do, to change yourself and the world! But you are a little stuck at the moment. Unfortunately, you are incarcerated, serving two life terms, to run consecutively. Life is so unfair. You are rotting in a jail cell when you could do so much on the outside. And of course, you are innocent. Well, maybe not exactly innocent, but not guilty of all of the things you were convicted of. Or things did not go the way they say they did. But, to make a long story short, you want out. The problem is that escapes do not usually work out.

To be clear, this author would never encourage or condone a prison escape (that is what the lawyers told us to write, anyway). By all means, do pay your debt to society, offer restitution, repent your sins, and pray for forgiveness. But, if not, here are some thoughts for you.

Prison breaks are quite common. In some cases, they even take place in maximum security prisons. Some escapes are simply done through bribery of prison officials while others are daring performances involving digging tunnels or climbing over impossible fences. There is no limit to the imagination of inmates who truly want to break free. Statistically, however, many escapees are caught within days of their escape, almost all of them in fact.

One reason for the high failure rate of escapes is that authorities do not like them. They make prison officials look bad, the police inefficient, and elected local officials incompetent. They all seem to hold a belief that those sent to prison should stay there. Another reason why escapees tend to be caught is bad planning. They spend months or years planning the details of the escape. They involve family or friends. They build alliances and spend their savings or ill-gotten gains to buy their way out. They do a detailed study of the facility. They assess the weak links in the security structure. They test the preparedness of prison officials. They conspire with their prison mates. Day after day, they work at their plan, strengthened by their dream of freedom. They are filled with a vision of a beautiful outside world and their old life, to which they think they can return. Unfortunately for them, however, things do not work that way.

Before you walk out of those gates or climb over the wall, know this: Authorities are going to come down on you "like a ton of bricks." They will throw at you everything they've got. In no time, they will have a profile on you, if they don't have one already. Your profile will include your picture, likes and dislikes, survival skills, past military experience, hunting or fishing licenses, and anything in your past that could help them predict your moves. They will have a list of your associates, relatives, and friends. They will track down all of your previous addresses, email addresses, and phone numbers. They will use security cameras, personnel, dogs, radio, thermal imaging, and informants. The police will put pressure on your loved ones, if you have any left. They will follow your known associates and friends hoping for a rendezvous with you.

This type of surveillance will go on for some time. Usually after about 6 months, if they have not found you, the trail goes cold but not dead. You will not be safe. Realistically, you are not going to get away unless you have a detailed plan, a Plan B.

Poof!

You slept late today, it's almost eleven in the morning. Somehow you did not hear the radio alarm, or it failed to go off. As soon as you look at the alarm clock, however, you notice something strange. While the clock is battery operated and seems to be in working order, the radio alarm, which is fed from the house power supply, seems to be down. You tinker with it a bit, but then it dawns on you: the power is out. Which is why there seems to be an eerie silence about the place. No humming of machinery, the refrigerator, or the heat pump that usually roars from the basement. You get up and go to the bathroom. But when you turn on the water, nothing happens. Maybe, you think, this could be connected to the power outage. It's too late to go back to bed, so you head for the kitchen to make some coffee. There is enough bottled water to make a cup or two. Oh, wait, without power, you can't make coffee.

While you are starting to get annoyed, you glance out the window, and what you see is downright shocking. There is an eerie silence everywhere. No cars seem to be going by. All you can see are groups of people gathered on the street and talking or whispering to each other. You have no idea what that is all about but grab your phone to see if you can get a news channel since the television will not work. The phone still has some charge, but it's dead: no signal. Could the power outage have also affected the cell towers? In a state of anxiety, you quickly dress and head down the stairs toward the street. You join a group of people already assembled there. They all seem to be in a state of confusion. They have heard rumors but no confirmation of what is causing the power, water, cell towers, and other systems to crash.

Soon enough, word starts to come in of a devastating attack on the country's infrastructure and power grid. Shortwave radio amateurs have relayed information from an underground facility. It appears that little North Korea, which had been flying satellites and testing nuclear devices, has finally made good on its threat to destroy the West. It exploded a large nuclear device, which it had loaded on one of its satellites, high above the atmosphere. The explosion created an EMP, or electromagnetic pulse. The effects have been catastrophic over a radius of 2,000 miles on the ground. Most super transformers have been destroyed, which means that not only is power out today but it will also not be restored for months or even years. Cell towers cannot operate because of a lack of power and neither can water pumps around the nation. Communications have been wiped out. Most cars, motorcycles, and buses do not run because their electronics have been fried by the magnetic pulse. Trains do not run. Food processing facilities are not going to be able to operate, let alone deliver products. Gas stations are closed, even if one were able to start a car. Cash machines are not operating. There seems to be no police anywhere in sight; and, therefore, no one to keep law and order. Stores are closed. Gas, heat, and electric appliances are not going to work. And it's still morning on a cold winter day.

You don't know what is going to happen next. But a cold and starving mob roaming the streets does not bode well for your lifestyle or, for that matter, your survival. You do have an old bicycle somewhere in the garage, and that may be a means of transportation. But it will not solve your problems. With a huge area affected by the calamity, it is not at all sure that you could, hungry and cold on a bike, reach safety. Furthermore, there will be mobs of people trying to get away. You would be riding chaotic and lawless roads. There will be armed people looting and robbing. But the biggest problem of all is that, even if you were able to get on the road, where would you go? With millions on the run, you would not be able to find lodging or even food. If you had a cabin in the woods somewhere, equipped for survival, that would make all of the difference. All you would need to do would be to reach the cabin, lock up, and load your (legally obtained) guns. But, alas, you never thought of this kind of need, did you? How much better your prospects would be if you had a Plan B!

A Self-Made Man

I was brought up in a blue-collar neighborhood of a large city. My parents were immigrants from Eastern Europe, and I practically grew up in my father's tailor shop. He was a hard-working man. In fact, he ended up working himself to death. No time off, no vacations, and saving every penny for the family. Through his hard work, my father was able to give me and my sister an education, so that our lives would be better than the one my parents had. In other words: I came from nothing. And a long way I have come! I am what they call a self-made man.

I inherited my father's work ethic. I believe in sacrifice and purpose. I want to do good for myself and others. But, as I watched my father toil in the shop, measuring customers' garments, cutting cloth, and sewing, I always thought that there must be a better way–a way to create more wealth with less labor. That is essentially what distinguishes man from animals–our brain and our tools. We create tools that we then employ to achieve what we need with less work than it would take for an animal without those tools. But my father did give me something that really helped me along the way: an education. I easily graduated from high school and then went on to study business. And that is where I really got my tools!

I am very proud of my accomplishments. I found a way to create wealth, immense wealth. While it is hard to calculate my net worth, I believe that I am worth close to one billion pounds sterling–billion with a "b"! Of course, I have enjoyed some creature comforts, but I have also spread my wealth. I have made many people happy and rich, or so I believed until recently. And I use the word "believe" in all its possibilities and power. I found out that there is no limit to the power of imagination, and that imagination can be reality if you want it to be.

Some people believe that in order to be and feel rich, you need to control brick and mortar or hold gold nuggets in your hand. I disagree with that old-fashioned way of thinking. In my view, the knowledge that you have financial power, that you can watch your wealth grow on a screen, can give a lot of pleasure. And there is no greater comfort than having a reputable company, such as the one I run, to manage your assets. For the past 15 years, I have been receiving investments from the public. My financial empire started with small investments from relatives and friends. I was able to offer better than average returns and, once word spread of my unique skills, the investors' pool began to grow exponentially.

In reality it is difficult, if not impossible, to offer returns on investment much greater than the competition because investment vehicle outputs, whether they be stocks, funds, currencies, derivatives, or metals, are pretty much determined by the market. But that is where I parted with old-fashioned investment thinking. My program involved investing clients' money in traditional ways but also supplementing the interest

I paid my clients by using funds coming in from new investors. And since a firm with my reputation can always expect to bring in new funds, I could benefit both myself and my clients with great returns. Of course, naysayers would label my program a Ponzi scheme, a system where one robs Peter to pay Paul. But my critics only speak out of envy. I am sure they secretly admire my genius and my enterprise. All they need to do is look at my happy customers, who care about one thing and one thing only: ever higher balances and returns. Why should they care about the details of how the income is generated? My clients are good people who save and invest. They are usually not financial gurus, and thank God for that!

A tool of my brilliant enterprise is image. That is in fact a very important aspect of my entire program. My clients must believe that I am doing very well, so that they will feel more confident in placing their saving with my firm and refer more investors. There is no better advertising than good performance and no better way of showing success than through a display of the usual trappings of wealth. Among my promotional tools is a yacht that I keep in Cannes, France. She is a wonderful boat, all 320 feet of her, with a beam of 50 feet and spectacular engines that power her to 32 knots. The interiors are lush and include nine guestrooms in addition to crew quarters. The living area is of superb quality, and it includes a proper sitting room in addition to a dining room that can seat 24. On decks, she is every bit as gorgeous as she is inside. An open deck is suitable for al fresco dining and cocktails. The upper deck has room for a helicopter, although we seldom use it. She was originally designed for an oil tycoon from the Gulf States. I bought her when she was almost new and have since embarked on a major refit, which added 20 million pounds to the original price of 160 million. That was money well spent because over the years I have been able to lavishly entertain my largest investors. We have gone on several Mediterranean cruises where champagne flowed freely and attractive hostesses entertained guests in style. In the future, we plan to extend these cruises to the Caribbean for the winter season so as not to interrupt the blessing that such a yacht can bestow on me and my clients. Regrettably, my wife has been ill for some time and cannot accompany me on these joyous excursions, but I manage to find many young women to assist me in entertaining my valued guests and myself.

The yacht is great for entertaining, but when I really need to move, there is nothing like my Gulfstream jet. That is another tool to display success and, therefore, attract ever more investments. And it is also very handy for quick trips to Dubai, New York, and other business destinations. I also entertain at home in what I call, if I may say so myself, a spectacular chateau. And, of course, I make sure that there are always in the driveway some fine motor cars to further impress guests.

Unfortunately, with all this travel and entertaining, I've come up a bit short in the actual investment of the funds that come from my clients. In fact, a big part of those funds is expended to maintain my homes, yacht, jet, and general lifestyle. I look at it as a cost of doing business. And my business consists primarily in promoting more business. I also have what you may call a pension plan. Every month at the embassy of a certain African nation in London, a small cargo of gold arrives via diplomatic pouch. We are talking gold in the raw, as in nuggets. Beautiful little pebbles that give me so much joy when I hold them in my hand. I buy everything that comes in and at a good price, as this gold comes straight from the mines. Some say this is like blood diamonds because the work conditions of the miners leave a little to be desired. But who am I to judge the operation of those mines? I am not a union president but just a happy customer.

I had originally planned to sell the gold on the regular market at retail prices. And the income from the sale would be directly reinvested in my financial program to pay dividends to investors, minus of course my expenses. But I thought I could do better than that. I have been sending the gold to some associates in Russia who use it to purchase small weapons for export. And guess where we are exporting to? Africa! So, we have created a magic loop for wealth creation that keeps the investors happy and the operation going. And while in Africa, I also started to diversify by branching off into the health business, namely the blood trade. It was a great idea to start the new business because I was capitalizing on synergies. My contacts in the African country that provides the gold are close to several tribal chiefs in villages. Those chiefs have been encouraging their population to donate blood. We have shipped several trailers equipped with top-of-the-line equipment to draw, test, and refrigerate blood. The blood is then sent to Europe, where it is sold for handsome profits. And I think all of that blood is doing a lot of good to those who need it. As long as they can pay for it, everybody wins.

All my operations make perfect financial sense, but some problems have come up. Some activists in Africa, and their representatives in Europe and America, have been digging into my business practices. They claim that the weapons we ship to Africa are being sold to child soldiers. And they claim that that violates a number of United Nations instruments as well as international treaties. As a financial person, I do not know much about warfare and even less about demographics. Who the end users of my products are, I do not know and, quite frankly, do not care to learn. I am guessing that children are plentiful in that part of the world, and they are probably fearless. So, they might make terrific soldiers, but what do I know? I buy, sell, and create wealth.

Another problem that has come up is that activists in Africa, maybe the same people who complain about the arms sales, are making an issue of the exploitation of the blood donors. That is so unfair! A donor is a donor, so there can be no exploitation, even if tribal chiefs do exert a little pressure on them. But that links back to the mines, where there seem to be concerns over safety and the minimum wage. Again, I am only a businessman and a very successful one. What do I know about prevailing working conditions in Africa or the rights of the local workforce?

These do-gooders who are causing so much trouble for my existing businesses in Africa are also trying to hamper my latest venture there: organ harvesting. The tribal chiefs who are so helpful in soliciting blood donations are also starting to collect organs from cadavers and even living donors. I am not too familiar with the particulars of this operation, but I can tell a great opportunity when I see one. And, most important, I can see how we can help sick patients in Switzerland and other European countries and beyond. We can cut the time they need to wait for an organ and maybe save their lives. I wish my father could see me now.

Unfortunately, the noise that these activists are generating about my business activities in Africa has triggered an interest in my financial operations in the UK, Europe, and America. Authorities have been looking into my business deals with a microscope. They are raising questions about the viability of my investment scheme. I have also been approached by two lawyers representing recent investors who are requesting an audit of their clients' accounts. All this is unprecedented and frightening. The fact of the matter is, I do not keep accurate records. Money comes in, and it goes out. My genius is in orchestrating the big picture, not in micro-managing accounts. And to be totally honest, I doubt that my numbers could hold up to scrutiny when the law comes knocking. Adding to all of my troubles, the recent tumble in the stock market has also made it difficult to balance the books. Not that I actually purchased that many stocks to begin with, because of all of the image and entertainment expenses. But now, for the first time in years, it appears that we have a gaping hole that cannot be filled without major infusions of cash from new investors. And the bad publicity, along with expected government investigations, will make sure that that is not going to happen.

I have discussed my problems with a lawyer, and he seems to be worried. He has asked me for a very large retainer. He also said to me or, rather, whispered that this may be a good time to take that long vacation I have been dreaming of; and, if I forgot to come back, so much the better. But he won't say much more. I am starting to get really worried. So here I am, still sitting on a huge pile of cash and gold with nowhere to go. If only I had a Plan B!

A Ghost's Regret

I am the ghost of Kim Jong Nam, speaking through the pen of this book's author. I was the stepbrother of Kim Jong-Un, the despotic ruler of North Korea. Before this book went to press, I was brutally murdered by agents of North Korea at Kuala Lumpur Airport. Two young women in the employ of my no-good brother approached me and wiped poison on my face. In a matter of hours, I was dead, and history was changed. I could have become the enlightened leader of North Korea. I could have transformed that sad little country into a prosperous Asian nation, all while I resided on board a fantastic mega yacht in Monaco.

Had I read "Plan B," I would be alive today to make the world a better place. I would have understood that booking a flight using an alias known to the North Korean government would place me at the Kuala Lumpur Airport. I would have understood that strangers, no matter how lovely, reaching for my face was a deadly threat. I could have used a different name. I could have made alternate reservations on different flights. I could have used private transportation. I could have lived in peace until the time was right to knock out my no-good brother. Oh, how I wish I had read this book!

A Very Private Man

My story is not unusual or unconventional. It is the ordinary tale of a midlife crisis that will not go away. I have talked to friends and have also considered seeing a psychotherapist. But, at the end of the day, I cannot even feel sorry for myself. I am married and have two teenage girls. I live in a neatly kept house in a middle-class neighborhood. I have a professional job but have not had much of a career. Time is marching on, and life is passing me by. I thought I did everything I was supposed to do. But now I have this deep feeling of frustration and, at times, even despair. To make a long story short, I think, in fact I am pretty sure, that my wife is cheating on me. Not only that, I don't even care. Sometimes I wish someone would get her off my back. Take her; you can have her and don't bring her back. My daughters do not love me. I don't mean that they hate me, but I feel an absence of love. And absence and silence can have a powerful impact.

I have thought a great deal about what I might do about my situation. I do not feel about *doing* anything in particular. I wish I could hide somewhere or become invisible. I wish I could just close my eyes and disappear. I wish I could use a paint brush to white out my life over the past 10 years. But that cannot be done. I must take some action that will get me away from the rut I am in. So, I have looked carefully at my employment situation. I have considered my financial means, the retirement account. I have thought about the education of my daughters. The more I look at all this, however, the more I become convinced that there is no practical way to disentangle myself from this mess without doing damage to the family I still love and who does not love me. I wish I had planned for an alternative years ago when things were good. Now I could just step out of this situation and get a new beginning, another roll of the dice. But, alas, I have no Plan B!

A Bishop's Prayer

Bless me father for I have sinned. To my fault, to my fault, to my most grievous fault.

I am a Catholic bishop in the twilight of my life, and I come from a long line of prelates. My life has been devoted to ministering to the sick and to the youth, sometime to wayward youth that needed to find their way to God and salvation. I have sacrificed my own lifestyle and comfort in order to bring the light to others. I have risen through the ranks from a lowly country priest to the upper echelons of the magnificent Church of Rome I now represent. What pride and joy I feel when I look back to decades of achievement and work to glorify God! I get tears in my eyes when I think of all of the lost souls I have saved from perdition and damnation.

Unfortunately, the dark forces of evil are now conspiring to end my work in the church. They are set to shut out the light I have brought to minds and communities in danger of perdition. The dark forces of the media, allied with the Devil, are out to get me. A newspaper in particular, run by atheist elements, is getting ready to start the dirty work. It is planning to publish interviews with no fewer than 72 minors who falsely claim that I have sought, and in many cases received, carnal knowledge of them. I have no recollection of those acts they claim I committed. Of course, my memory is not as good as it used to be, and sometimes I am a bit confused by the beneficial effects of church wine, but I am sure there is no truth to those base allegations.

The atheist media is also accusing me of improper accounting practices during my work with the Vatican Bank. They falsely allege that a few million euros are missing from the accounts I handled. Those accusations deeply hurt me. But even worse are the accusations that I have sold indulgences to wealthy parishioners. I do not recall specific transactions with parishioners. But one should keep in mind that indulgences are very valuable to those who truly seek salvation. And if you look at it from that point of view, the only accurate point of view, what is a little bit of money compared with eternal salvation? And, considering today's inflation and the rising cost of living, how much is 100,000 euros really worth? For someone who has been blessed with financial success in this life, is it not prudent to invest some of the gains in the afterlife? Should one not hedge their bets as they start walking into the sunset? And what better way is there to repay the Lord's blessings than with a donation to the Church or their appointed servants?

But I digress. No matter what anyone says, it is clear to me that a conspiracy is in place, not only against me but against all people of faith. The atheists of the world, along with their communist allies, are seeking to take over society as we know it. They are planning to replace it with an undignified secular model that serves only the greed and selfishness of political elites. They are planning a world where abortion, euthanasia, and all manner of sexual perversions are glorified and are going to be the pillars of the new order. As a leader of the Church, I am a natural target, but I will defend myself through the power of the Lord.

On my knees, I close my eyes and pray:

"Dear Lord, maker of heaven and earth, please save your humble servant from the tentacles of the Devil. Do not let the forces of evil prosper from their ungodly crusade against me and the Church. If I have sinned, I repent. But while my whole being is oriented toward Heaven, I also need, during what little time I have left in this valley of tears, your guidance to a temporary haven for myself and my meager savings. Please Lord do not permit that my enemies and Your enemies pierce the corporate veil of my Bahamian companies. Let them not extend their greedy and bloodthirsty hands to my Cayman accounts. Most of all, Lord, I pray that you will save my Panama foundation, which I have built over the years as a safeguard against the dark days when the Church would come under attack. For my benefit, maybe, but mostly for Your glory. I tremble, my Lord, at the thought of the foundation's demise. Because if the Devil takes down the foundation, with it all else will come down like a house of cards. All exposed like low-hanging fruit ready to be stolen. And I pray, my Lord and Savior, that you can show me the way out of this cruel country and into a safe place, under the sun, where I can continue Your work. Please give me a plan, Lord, a Plan B. So I pray. Amen."

Moral of the Story

One can imagine many situations in which it might be desirable to get away, disappear, or maybe just drop under the radar for a while. The details of every situation are different, and yet, every scenario has one thing in common: the need for a plan. Whatever your station and situation in life, changes are difficult. Life is full of entanglements and complications. Money, business, jobs, habits, family, and personal relationships all play a role in making decisions. Making decisions on the spur of the moment and under pressure usually leads to failure. Detailed preparations are not possible, mistakes are made, and one can find herself in the unenviable position of not being able to go forward or go back. The time to repair a roof is not when it pours but when the sun is out. The same is true for insurance. You don't try to get fire insurance when the house is burning. If you are ever going to make a Plan B, the time is now, just after you're done reading this book!

There is another advantage in having a Plan B when you do not need it. The fact of the matter is that most people never need "to go to ground" or "fly under the radar." Most people live their lives inside the box where they have been placed or which they have created for themselves—quiet, ordinary lives without any conflict or drama, without even a thought of an alternative life somewhere else. In fact, even the thought of disappearing is uncommon. Some will say these are plans for criminals or spies. Yet, there are situations in life where one could benefit from having at least the *option* of sliding into an alternative life plan. Even if in the end one chooses to stay put and fight whatever life throws at you, the mere thought of having that alternative, of the possibility to run to a better place, can make you so much more powerful in dealing with the challenges facing you. And then, you may not need to run after all.

TWO

SURROUNDED

F ollowing the predicament of the previous imaginary
characters, we are now going to get down to real-life
details. This chapter focuses on common vulnerabilities
for privacy-conscious individuals. We are trying to give a
sense of reality and context in the effort to counter the various
threats to privacy and individual freedom. For the purposes
of this summary, we will deal with threats individually. In
later chapters, however, it will become apparent how big
and crushing the cumulative impact of all of these attacks
on privacy can be.

I. Who Is Looking

Before we deal with the list of items that can threaten
privacy or security, it is important to determine who the
opposition is and its strength. If we are talking about a jealous husband, it is one thing. But if you are a deposed dictator
running with a bag full of diamonds, the challenges are vastly
different. The stronger and better financed the opposition,
the tougher it is to hide. If you are running from a powerful
government, your life is going to be very difficult and possibly

shorter than you would like it to be. The government of a large nation can bring to bear money, intelligence, organizations like Interpol, cooperation from other governments, and many other tools that can render an escape very problematic.

Dealing with low-level opposition requires the employment of tools detailed in this book as well as many others explained in various technical publications available in bookstores and online. It also requires experience and common sense, which may or may not be intuitive. Defending from powerful governments, however, is very, very difficult if not impossible. You would need a lot of money, a lot of luck, and the ability to adapt to a simple life under the radar. A case in point was that of Osama bin Laden, probably the most wanted man in decades, who managed to evade capture for many years. What is known about his life in hiding is that he avoided the use of email, phones, and just about every electronic gadget that most people in modern society rely on. He may also have bought protection from a local government in Pakistan. He used couriers for all communications and exchanges. He seldom, if ever, left his compound and was in effect neutralized as the leader of his terrorist organization.

In the end, Osama bin Laden may have been sold out by one of his lieutenants who was impressed by the $25 million bounty. One can imagine the internal anguish of the lieutenant as he considered the pros and cons of betraying his boss and leader. On the one hand, the lieutenant may have reasoned, bin Laden was a pious man of great political accomplishment and a great leader for many Muslims around the world. On the other hand, one had to consider the rising cost of living, the dusty environment, and limited infrastructure that threatened the proper upbringing of children in the compound. And then there may have been the brochures of villas on Lake Geneva and Caribbean hideaways that seemed to offer so much to a family man of faith. In the end, the lieutenant probably went for the bounty, which goes to show that $25 million has a way to shake the deepest friendship bond and the strongest faith. And if things went that way, then you can see how far a major country can go in pursuit of the people it is seeking.

2. Vulnerabilities

Main Identifiers

Your Name

Yes, your name is a problem. It is listed in multitudes of databases as well as on your ID documents. It is the single most common identifier among public records, social connections, and many consumer and commercial activities. The section on identities will offer some ideas on possible alternatives to your old self.

Your Date of Birth

Along with your name, your date of birth nails your identity, ruling out virtually any possibility of confusing you with another person with the same or similar name. Assuming, of course, that fake documents are not involved.

Your Face

Remember when you went to renew your driver's license and they had you stand in front of a camera? That was a digital photo for your license. Of course, the Department of Motor Vehicles has that photo, but you may wonder who else has it or can obtain it. Here is a partial and painful summary: local and federal agencies, including intelligence agencies; the police; Interpol; foreign governments and all of their agencies; and private investigators and their clients. Have you ever heard of facial recognition technology? It's nasty stuff. The software allows comparisons of a stored picture with multiple images taken from, say, social media or even shot on the street by automated cameras or manned cameras. Someone can take a picture of a person, at a street rally for example. If they have access to a digital photo of the target, they can run a search of DMV databases for a match. If a match is achieved, then authorities (or whoever can get access to the database) can determine the identity of the person at the rally. It gets worse. Software long employed by governments, and now available to consumers, can perform a comparison search of a given picture (your driver's license picture, for example) against the universe of pictures on the Internet. Depending on the matches, the search can tell the investigator where else the picture of the person is found on the Internet. That could reveal where the person has been. Conversely, by taking a picture of an individual on the street or using an image from the Internet, a search can link to the person's ID on a government database.

Your National ID Number, Social Security Number, or Whatever Number Your Country Uses To Collect Taxes and Pay Out Benefits

That number most of the time is used in connection with bank accounts, credit applications, and all related transactions. It describes your credit risk based on your past consumer activities, loan repayment history, present and past addresses, purchasing habits, and many other things.

ID Cards and Passports

Modern passports and national ID cards are embedded with radio frequency identification chips that can transmit data over a short distance. Those chips pose a major threat to someone's privacy because of the many ways the information extracted from them can be used.

Fingerprints

As will be explained in more detail in the chapter on forensics, human fingerprints are detailed, difficult to alter, and almost unique. They are durable over the life of an individual. That is why they are employed as long-term markers of identity. Those who are in possession of your fingerprints can use them to compare with prints you may have left on a glass or other surface and, therefore, place you on a given date in a given place. Even if you have no criminal records, the chances are that you have been fingerprinted through job applications, hunting license applications, gun permit applications, and many other situations in which the individual comes into contact with the government.

DNA

DNA, short for deoxyribonucleic acid, is a polymer that carries genetic instructions for the development, functioning, growth, and reproduction of all known organisms and many viruses. Forensic scientists and, for what concerns this book, the opposition can use DNA in blood, semen, skin, saliva, or hair found at a crime scene to identify a matching DNA of an individual, such as a perpetrator or a fugitive. Unfortunately, there is nothing you can do to change your DNA.

Other Vulnerabilities

Credit Cards

Like other banking instruments, credit cards are loaded with information about you and can be stolen or hacked.

Credit card chips can emit radio-frequency identification signals that can be skimmed. A breach of your credit card can lead to identity theft, among other things.

Store Discount Cards

These harmless-sounding cards actually pack a big punch. In order to get one, you need to fill out an application form. You could have applied for one years ago and forgotten all about it. But the information is all there. Your name, date of birth, address, and phone number. But what the card does is that, by tricking you into using it by offering small discounts, it captures your purchasing patterns. Your purchases can tell a lot about you, like your lifestyle, income, state of health, travel patterns, family status, or living arrangements. The real damage to your privacy takes place when that information is integrated with all of the additional data available about you in other databases, government and private.

Real Estate and Address

Whether you own or lease, your address is going to end up in multiple databases which, in turn, sell or transfer that information to many other data consolidators for use by multitudes of merchants, advertisers, and others. Your address can be interesting not only to locate you physically, but also to determine which merchandise you may be interested in buying or which people you may want to meet or date. It can provide a lead to where you may want to look for a job, apply for a loan, open a bank account, join a club, explore new restaurants, visit a doctor, or buy a burying plot. If you live with family or friends, your address will also link to those close to you. All of that information can be cross-checked by a people search. Even if your house is in your spouse's name, a search on him or her will link to you.

If you have a lease on a property, the chances are they have checked your credit by using your tax ID number. That credit check is going to be part of your record. If the opposition is checking your credit history, they will find that you have applied for a rental in a given location and that would be an easy clue as to your address. In addition, the rental company may also have verified your previous address and references, another link in the history of your movements. When you sign the lease, you will also be filling out forms and providing other information such as banking information. All of that data is normally kept on file by the rental company. These days such files may be digital or even on the cloud, but more about that later.

If you purchase a property and you obtain a mortgage on it, the bank application alone contains dozens of pages full of your information. Practically your entire life will be divulged to the bank and, through them, to anyone who can access their files. That includes all government agencies and practically any private investigator worth "half his salt." Even if you do not get a mortgage and purchase the property in cash, there will still be a record of the transaction, care of the title company, notary, or whoever performs title searches and recording in your jurisdiction. If, God forbid, you are taking title in your own name, a title search will reveal that you own that property and be a clue to your address. It will also expose your asset to any lawsuit. In fact, the more assets you hold in your name, the more likely you are to get sued.

Utilities

Utilities are usually connected to an address. If those utilities are under your name, that is yet another link to where you live. In addition, if you are signing up for Internet, the

Internet provider is a major gateway to your online life. And since the Internet provider identifies an address, that address is where you would be expected to live or spend time.

Mail

Mail is another major liability for the privacy-conscious individual. For one thing, if you receive a significant amount of mail, the postman is bound to notice or remember your name. Maybe you even run into him on the street. He will then have a name *and* a face. More ominous still is the fact that the post offices can have digital records of deliveries, sometimes digital pictures of envelopes. Even the sender's address can be on file if it is shown on the outside of the envelope. Delivery of packages by courier companies are in a whole league of their own: They are like a nuclear blast on your address privacy. If you have received mail or special deliveries with your name on it, your only option to regain your privacy is to move.

Insurance

As we explain below, car insurance and car insurance claims are a major pitfall on the road to privacy. Health insurance is also highly problematic because any time it is used, it generates a lot of data. It ties in with a doctor's office, hospitals, pharmacies, and everything in between. All your prescriptions are in the system: what you are taking, how often, and where you buy it. Renter's insurance creates an obvious link between you and your address. Home insurance is normally required if you have a mortgage on the house. If you own your house free and clear, then it is worth thinking about going without it and self-insuring. As to life insurance, forget about it. If you are reading this book, you are probably past caring about what happens after you are gone.

Cars and Other Vehicles

Driving a car is a major liability for those who are looking for anonymity. In order to drive a car or a motorcycle, you need to register and insure it. In most jurisdictions, that now applies also to mopeds (small motorcycles under 50 cc). Registration requires your full identity, or that of a company, with a person's name for the record. Registration will normally be for an address that matches your driver's license. Insurance companies will also want to know where the vehicle is kept and operated. They will want to know who operates it (you?) and the driving history of that person. If you buy a vehicle on credit, to all of that information you must add your credit history. Taken together, all of the above items can readily identify you to the world.

If you have ever been stopped by the police while driving, you may have noticed that they approach you and then go back to their patrol car where they sit for a few minutes. On their part, that is time well spent. They can look up your plate number and find out your name, address, any aliases, outstanding warrants, and lots of other information that can guide their approach to the stop. If you are wanted for a serious crime and deemed armed and dangerous, for example, you can expect a rough ride when they come back to talk to you. If you have been wise enough to hide your address, an accident or police stop may doom your attempts to protect your privacy. If you are arrested for driving under the influence, the arrest will bring many problems with it, like your being fingerprinted, for example. More ominous still, new technologies are now beginning to be employed by local law enforcement agencies that enable the automated reading of license plates. Those technologies allow law enforcement, and anyone else with access, to follow the movement of citizens and their vehicles in ways that were not possible until recently. EZ pass readers, the automated toll collection machines installed at the entrance of certain highways, can also read your plate as well as connect directly with your credit card. To understand the full picture of intrusion on people's privacy, you should view these technologies in conjunction with other means of surveillance such as mobile phones that can track people by showing location, direction of movement, and speed.

For the privacy-conscious person, motor vehicles present other challenges as well. The opposition can attach a location device to your car, which is very hard to spot unless you are specifically looking for it. That device can easily lead any followers to wherever you are going, or back to your house. If you have managed to somehow hide your physical address, that would then be blown as you are followed to your house. If the opposition is dangerous and means to do you harm, they could rig the car with explosives set to go off either on ignition or through a remote control or timer. If they have done a shoddy job, you might be able to spot it before getting in the car. The telltale signs are usually loose wires or a tool left under the car. But, unless you are specifically looking for that and in luck, the chances are you would miss it.

Airline and Other Travel

Due to terrorism and other security issues, airline travel is as far from being anonymous as one can possibly get. When you buy a ticket, you need to provide your name and address. If you buy your ticket in cash, you are raising a red flag. But by buying it with a credit card, you are providing lots of additional information about yourself. When the time comes to check in, whether in person or online, you are asked for ID information as well as your date of birth. Make no mistake about it, the government has a database of all of your airline travel for the past decades. Not only do they know all of the flights you have taken in the past decades, but also who you were sitting next to. The reason for that is simple. If you fly from Dubai to Moscow and happen to be sitting next to a suspected terrorist, that could be a coincidence because on a plane there are hundreds of passengers. But, if a few months later you are flying, say, from Sydney to Hong Kong and are sitting next to the same person, that is no longer a coincidence: It is a connection.

The data collected by airlines and taken over by the government goes far beyond travel information. The government has so much information on international travelers that any flight you take adds to the already voluminous data the government has on you and is a devastating breach of your privacy. General aviation is still slightly less controlled. But the pilot should still file a flight plan, even if he changes his mind right above a dirt strip in the middle of nowhere. And, unless he "forgets" to do it, he should provide a flight manifest listing all crew and passengers on board. Even assuming that your pilot is very mindful of your private concerns, can you trust her? What is to stop her from selling you out?

The moral of the story is that if you want to travel anonymously, flying is definitely not the way. Forget flying completely. There can be exceptions if you are using a total new identity that is set in stone. But travel to certain countries requires a visa and/or fingerprints, and that would take down your whole setup. Of course, this book does not recommend any practice that is illegal, but see the chapter on identities for more information.

Travel by train is of different types. In developed countries and traveling on high-speed or first-class trains, you need to provide ID and usually pay by credit card. Regional trains can be more informal, and you can usually pay in cash at the station without ID. Some people board those trains without a ticket and pay the fare plus a fine during the trip, if they are caught. Buses tend to follow the same pattern as trains but are usually more informal, unless you book and pay online.

Children's Schools

Like it or not, your child's school is a major impediment to maintaining an anonymous existence. And an even bigger obstacle if you are seeking a quiet departure from your area. The reason for that is that school records are very extensive and include not only the child's address but also information about parents, medical issues, previous addresses, and a plethora of other details. If you relocate, it would then be necessary to find a school in the new area. But any school, public or private, would want to see school records from the schools previously attended by the children. If the opposition were looking for you and knew you were traveling with children, it would be very simple to track you down. A person planning a discreet move would do well to consider the homeschooling option, far in advance of the intended date of departure.

Medical Care

Hopefully you are feeling well and will continue to be in good health. If not, bear in mind that a visit to the doctor can not only be painful and expensive but can also put a major hole in your privacy strategy. If you are using health insurance, as we pointed out earlier, a visit to the doctor can generate a monumental amount of data cruising through multiple computers. It would take this entire chapter to begin listing the things that are generated with an insurance claim. Doctors and hospitals also keep records and lots of them. In turn, they communicate information to your favorite pharmacy (near your house?). Opposition forces *love* medical records. Those records can say a lot about you–not only your general state of health and any medical conditions you may have but also your medication purchasing patterns. If you need to buy medications on a regular basis, your main residence and travels may be revealed by what you buy and when. Even if you pay in cash, there is still going to be a record of the doctor's prescription. And if you buy a lot of medication and then stop buying it for a while, that could be an indication that you are traveling or have moved. Your medical conditions may also give clues to the path you are likely to take in the event you are trying to make yourself scarce. In fact, certain conditions will rule out a whole set of destinations. If you need regular dialysis, for example, you are unlikely to head for a jungle or stay there long. If your main issue is rheumatism, it is unlikely that you would be heading for Siberia, or at least not of your own will, anyway.

Computers, Laptops, Tablets, Telephones, and Other Gadgets

This area is a minefield. While new technologies can offer many advantages and opportunities, including for someone who wants to fly under the radar, life is more complicated than it used to be. Protecting your devices from theft and intrusion is a major job that requires expertise and diligence. All it takes is one slip, and your game is up. The issues presented by technology can essentially be divided into two areas: hardware and software.

Protecting your devices from theft is accomplished by using common sense and old-fashioned techniques. Do not leave your devices unattended; do not ship them; do not let them out of your sight; and, whenever possible, lock them. Several safety devices are on the market, including cables. Unlike a watch or other precious item, laptops and other electronic devices not only can be stolen but can also be compromised. Someone with nefarious intentions who gains access to your computer can copy files or install malware that can make it do things you would rather it not do. Spying software installed on a laptop, for example, can activate a webcam and have it take snapshots of what is in front of it, such as the user, and watch her. Of course, it helps if you digitally lock a device, but while it may deter a casual thief from doing mischief, it will not stop a professional.

By far the biggest liability for the privacy-conscious individual is the smartphone. For one thing, phone communications are relatively easy to intercept. But there is another ominous problem. A mobile phone is a location positioning device. If you ever turn on the Global Positioning System (GPS) function on a Google phone, the following statement appears:

"Let Google's location service help apps find your location quickly and accurately, which can reduce battery consumption. Anonymous location data will occasionally be sent to Google, even when no apps are running."

Ouch! The system then provides you with two options: "agree" or "disagree." If you choose the agree option, your consent becomes a permanent default on the phone you are using. If you disagree, you will be asked that question every time you turn on the GPS. The sad thing is that whatever you choose, the phone will locate you anyway. If you have any doubts, try turning off the location features and then call a tow truck company from the phone. No matter what, they will have your exact location. And if a private tow truck company can automatically get your location, you can imagine the possibilities of unwanted pursuers getting that information.

There are several ways in which a phone can track your location. The GPS function is one. Then there is the cell tower network. By triangulating the information sent to and from the towers, the system can track your location pretty accurately. Another way for a phone to track you is through wireless networks. As you walk down the street, you normally pass next to establishments that have wireless service. Your phone can see them, and they can see it. A database of wireless locations can serve as a map to follow your movements. If your phone is turned off, these tracking systems should not work. Unless you think the phone is off but, through installed malware, it is actually on. You may have some luck by removing the battery or keeping the phone in what is known as a Faraday cage, or at least wrapped in aluminum foil. But then there is no point in carrying a phone.

A television that can watch you or record you? You bet. The future is already here. Recent revelations from WikiLeaks, for example, contain documents explaining how some smart TV models, the ones that are connected to the Internet, can record voices in the room and transmit them over the Internet to the snoopers. Even when you think the TV is off, installed malware can actually keep the TV on to record and transmit.

Tempest

Tempest (Telecommunications Electronics Materials Protected From Emanating Spurious Transmissions) is a NATO and U.S. National Security Agency specification/certification referring to spying on information systems through leaking emanations. Those emanations include

GD Applegate

unintentional radio or electrical signals, vibrations, and sounds. Tempest refers to both spying on others and protection from such spying. The scope of Tempest spying is both chilling and mind boggling. It can include logging a user's keystrokes using motion sensors inside smartphones. Emissions may thus be intercepted and analyzed thereby revealing information transmitted, received, or processed by any type of equipment. Equipment protection measures from Tempest spying include shielding, filtering, masking, and distance. This is a technical field, and much of it is classified. But it should be just another reminder of the vulnerability of any information-processing device.

Pegasus and Similar Malware

Pegasus spyware was designed by a cyber-intelligence company to access sensitive information on the devices of suspected terrorists and other individuals considered undesirable by certain states. Pegasus spyware can infect an iPhone or Android device without any action from the target, and it can track phone calls, location, text messages, and emails. Pegasus spyware infects the target's phone without the need for the target to click a link or take any other action. Once installed on an Android or iOS device, Pegasus can secretly monitor and collect private data by reading text messages and emails, accessing the microphone and camera, listening in on phone calls, recording passwords, and tracking the phone's location. The information Pegasus collects is then uploaded to cloud servers for storage and analysis. Originally developed as a tool to combat terrorism, the spyware has been used to hack the phones of journalists, activists, and major politicians. There are other similar malware systems available to governments around the world and, increasingly, also to private companies. Depending on who you are or what you do, dear reader, someday they could target you.

The country of Israel was recently able to blow up pagers belonging to members of Hezbollah in Lebanon. Of course, the pagers were not ordinary issue but replacements Israel had arranged to be delivered to certain customers in Lebanon. Nevertheless, that operation showed how vulnerable phones and other mobile gadgets can be to malign operators.

Dataminr and Other Artificial Intelligence Companies

These companies are used by corporations to monitor events in real time and help with crisis response, but they can also be used for social media intelligence. They allow users to analyze conversations, synchronize social signals, and synthesize social data points into meaningful trends and analysis. It's not hard to see how intrusive this social media intelligence can be.

Internet and Email

In addition to the vulnerability of electronic devices, the Internet itself presents many dangers but also offers many opportunities for those trying to evade detection. It is sad to see how a technology that could have liberated billions of people is now turning into a major tool of repression. The focus of this chapter is only to give you some ideas as to how your data can be obtained by third parties, with or without your consent, and how your privacy is under constant attack. The scope of the discussion here is limited, however, as the field is extremely complex.

Most people believe that the greatest threat to online privacy comes from the National Security Agency (NSA) of the United States and corresponding specialized agencies around the world, such as the British GCHQ. That may in fact be true, but many local governments around the world are also acquiring online surveillance technology. And private merchants are also busy tracking your online activities. The typical intrusion into your online activity begins when you access a website. The minute you open a site, the site records your visit and passes on your information to other merchants, usually advertisers or data consolidators. For example, if you are looking at reviews of a sports car, your information might include: 1) your location; 2) your probable demographics and income level; 3) an interest in automobiles and, particularly, sports cars, and other general identifiers.

The way commercial tracking is done is usually through the use of cookies, which are small files planted on the personal computers or smart phones of those accessing a website. There is ad-blocking software that one can install to disable cookies, but that generally prevents normal browsing, and it is not believed to always work. In practice, in the end, you are forced to allow some tracking by these merchants. Not only does the website you are visiting track you, as you browse and shop online, the merchant you are visiting allows other companies and advertisers to monitor you, such as AddThis, Bazaarvoice, BlueKai, Coremetrics, Google, and many others. In addition to advertisers, those companies include data miners, analytics companies, ad auction companies, and consumer profilers.

If you do a search online on yourself, you may be shocked to learn that most information about you is readily available for sale. Current and old addresses, phone number, date of birth, social security number, criminal records, banking information, asset information, court records, list of relatives, and other biographical details. All that is the work of hundreds of data brokers that often work in tandem. In theory, one can "opt out" of the various databases, but that would be a monumental task destined to fail. For one thing, any request for opt-out involves paying money and filling out forms (yes, providing more information about yourself and usually your credit card information as well). Some sites will cooperate and others will not. Even for the sites that will comply with suppression, you may find that a search done through a foreign Internet provider may still show the information. And the data may remain cached somewhere from where it could be retrieved by a serious investigator.

The so-called Internet Wayback Machine is an enormous database archive established in 2006 and doubling in size about every year. It contains old web pages that are no longer active, those that have been deleted, and any history on those pages. It is of course searchable. Once the information is out, therefore, and it is for most of us, it is virtually impossible to erase it. All of the data available on the open Internet, combined with the massive amount of data collected by online merchants, can create an extensively detailed profile about most people on the planet.

Social Media

Strangers, with a few clicks of the mouse, can find out where we live; how old we are; how much money we make; where we shop; our sexual orientation; and our taste in cars, clothes, perfumes, and many other things. And if that were not enough, consider that many people choose to join social networks to add *even more* information and their pictures to the public domain. Facebook, X, Linkedin, Instagram, Tik Tok, and many other sites absorb data from billions of people and publish it to the world. Not only do people voluntarily add their pictures to Facebook and other sites, but their "friends" can also do that as well. And so, many lives are thus shared with friends and strangers in an interconnected universe. Some enjoy being "connected" and like to share as much of their private lives as possible. But that sometimes can be a problem. A few years ago, a married man had an affair and, during a long weekend, traveled with his lover to a resort. Upon returning home, he posted pictures of his trip on his Facebook page. Shortly afterward, the wife found out about the affair by accessing his Facebook page and filed for divorce. Her reasons for seeking a divorce allegedly were two: 1) the husband had been unfaithful, and 2) he was really stupid.

We have discussed above how face recognition technology can expose a person to unwanted scrutiny by those with access to digital photo IDs. But an official picture could be out of date and not render accurately the person's current look. By posting many online pictures to social networks, you add ammunition to the opposition. They then not only have an official photograph from your passport or driver's license but also various photos of yourself and your friends from your social activities. Those pictures can show the clothes you wear, your shoes, your eyewear, the locations you frequent, and even your body language vis-à-vis other persons in your group, as well as any pets you might have. Details about your friends, whether written or photographic, can also say a lot about your own life and your plans for the future. Of course, many people choose to use a nickname on their online profiles. But that is a very thin disguise that can be defeated by even the most basic investigator.

In addition to the social media sites where people share details of their life by posting pictures, videos, and text, there are sites where activities are actually organized. Meetup.com, for instance, has local chapters in just about every major city in the world. You select the city where you live and the topic that interests you, and you can usually find a number of local meetups. By joining, you find out about gatherings in that location on the topic of interest. If, for example, you live in Christchurch, New Zealand, and want to participate in groups that practice yoga, all you need to do is join that local meetup and sign up for any upcoming gathering. Sounds nice? Well, it is, but here's the downside. Let's say you live in the suburbs and sign up for a meetup downtown that takes place at a given café from 7 p.m. to 9 p.m. Someone who tracks your social activities knows that at 8 p.m. you are probably going to be downtown, so if they are interested in conducting a private visit of your home without your permission that is a good time to do it. Conversely, if the opposition is looking to get close and personal with you, they know that around 7 p.m. you will be heading for the downtown café and leaving it at 9 p.m. That could be a great opportunity for them but perhaps not for you.

3. Surveillance

Surveillance can take different forms and be conducted by government agents or private parties. Most discussions on surveillance tend to focus on Internet, phone, and other devices that represent recent technologies. But few activities can be more intrusive and unsettling than human surveillance, that is people observing and following you in person. It can be done by the police, private detectives, or angry ex-spouses. If professionals are following you, it's very hard to tell because they can use many tricks. Usually, multiple operatives will take turns and switch at various points while being directed by a control operative that runs the surveillance. That form of surveillance should be very much on the mind of the person attempting to disappear or conduct activities that she wishes to maintain private.

Gait Pattern Recognition Technology

Gait recognition is used to identify individuals in image sequences by the way they walk. In general, it works like this. Video sequences captured by different cameras are used as input, and then a human 3D model is set up. The motion is tracked by applying a local optimization algorithm. The motion trajectories of lower limbs are used as dynamic features. Finally, linear time normalization is used for matching and recognition. It is not difficult to see how this technology, along with imaging data sourced from available photographs, can help to identify individuals.

Radar

In addition to the well-known uses of radar by the police and the military, a new generation of devices is being deployed by police forces. Those devices allow the police to effectively peer through the walls of houses to see whether anyone is inside. Those radars work like sophisticated motion detectors, using radio waves to zero in on movements as slight as human breathing from a distance of over 50 feet. Not only can they detect whether anyone is in the house but also where they are and whether they are moving.

Drones

Drones are capable of highly advanced surveillance and can carry various types of equipment, including live-feed video cameras, infrared cameras, heat sensors, and radar. They can be deployed not only by the multiple agencies of government but also by private parties. Someone could station a drone in front of a window to take snapshots or footage. That may or may not be legal, but it would be hard for a private citizen to timely eliminate the threat before it does serious damage.

Aircraft

The use of aircraft for surveillance is not new. But, according to various reports, the U.S. Federal Bureau of Investigation (FBI) is operating a small air force with scores of low-flying planes across the United States, carrying video and also mobile phone surveillance technology. It should be noted that flight missions are usually undertaken without court approvals. In order to protect its operations, the planes are registered to front companies so that a quick check of the registration number would not give away the government connection. And, of course, to read the registration number, you would need to have access to the hangar or other storage location of the aircraft. Presumably, this use of aircraft can be accomplished by any sizable and well-equipped agency in the world.

Eyes in the Sky

There are many governments and commercial entities that operate satellites. The American agencies that make the most use of satellites are the Department of Defense (DOD), the Central Intelligence Agency (CIA), the National Security Agency (NSA), the National Reconnaissance Organization (NRO), and the National Geospatial Intelligence Agency (NGA). Also private companies such as Iridium and Inmarsat, among others, can capture and sell satellite imagery. Other countries that have placed satellites in orbit include Russia,

China, France, Japan, India, Canada, Israel, and North Korea. Military satellites are designed to move in elliptical orbit around the earth, and they can photograph large areas and determine the source of certain transmissions. Satellites may also be positioned in a geostationary orbit and stay relatively motionless. Geostationary satellites are employed to produce very detailed photographic imaging of important locations and to gather intelligence and eavesdrop on certain transmissions. Military operators also use geostationary satellites to precision-guide weapons to the intended target.

For what concerns you, an innocent person heading for the Land of the Disappeared, satellites are nasty things. If you are out in the open, they can see you and identify your car model and color if you are driving. If you are hidden in a hut, satellites can read your thermal signature from miles away. They can use a laser to bounce off windows and detect vibrations to reconstruct speech. To better understand your predicament if you are trying to run, you should view this technology in conjunction with other law enforcement tools.

K-9 Teams

A police dog team, known in some English-speaking countries as K-9 or K9, features a dog that is specifically trained to assist law enforcement personnel in their work. Their primary duties include searching for drugs and explosives, looking for crime scene evidence, and protecting their handlers. But these dogs can also be put to use in searching for a missing person or someone on the run. These animals have a phenomenal sense of smell and can track very efficiently. Some dog breeds, such as the German Shepherd, have many qualities that make them suitable for the job. They are usually male and not neutered so as to maintain their aggressive character.

Coast Guard Surveillance

The U.S. Coast Guard has traditionally been used for search and rescue and law enforcement, especially to interdict drug shipments. Post-9/11, however, some of the Coast Guard functions have shifted. It has created a data communication system to give pilots an active role in vessel tracking. The new technology is housed in an airborne small device that resembles a black box. Inside the box is an onboard computer and modem with a built-in Global Positioning System. This new system allows pilots to relay information from the air to the ground in less than a minute.

Thermal Imaging

Just in case you are planning some activity in the dark, hoping to avoid detection, think again. Thermal imaging is a sophisticated and non-invasive technique that utilizes infrared technology to detect heat emissions from various objects. This process converts the infrared energy, which is invisible to the human eye, into a visible light display. The infrared (IR) energy, or thermal energy, is emitted by all objects above absolute zero temperature, and the variations in these emissions form the basis of thermal imaging. Some viewing devices can see a human from a considerable distance.

LIDAR

LIDAR is an acronym for "light detection and ranging." It is a method for detecting ranges by targeting a surface or object with a laser and measuring the time for the reflected light to return to the receiver. This technology has terrestrial, airborne, and mobile applications.

Closed-Circuit Television (CCTV)

Last, but not least, in this brief summary of surveillance tools are closed-circuit television (CCTV) cameras. Those devices can be either video cameras or digital still cameras and are used for surveillance or other private purposes. They can be employed on city streets; and in bars, restaurants, stores, supermarkets, and banks. Advanced forms of CCTV, which utilize digital recorders, can record and store years' worth of recordings. In some large cities, police set up centralized surveillance centers where officers can view thousands of video cameras that essentially blanket the entire center of the city. The extensive use of this type of surveillance can create institutional abuse, abuse for private purposes, and illegal use by criminal elements that gain access to the footage provided by the cameras. The use of infrared technology also allows these cameras to see and record human activity that would normally be next to invisible to the naked eye in the dark.

The huge impact of these technologies can be understood only if seen in conjunction with other forms of surveillance. If, for example, you are doing what you hope is anonymous online research in a public locale with open Wi-Fi, CCTV footage could nail you. Let's say, for instance, that you are a suspected whistle blower attempting to research illegal practices of a company you work for and are trying to conduct sensitive communications away from your Internet server. If the company is on to your activity but has not narrowed down the culprit, they could acquire access to the CCTV footage (easy) from the store where the Wi-Fi communications in question seem to originate. They would then have images of the people using their computers at a given hour on a given date.

THREE

PRIVACY DEFENSE STRATEGIES

To put things in perspective, a general discussion is in order here. The discussion is central to the main theme of this book, as our thrust differs from privacy strategies that have been written by others in the past. In essence, we are going to bypass the many technical solutions that are offered in other books on privacy. The reason for this is that, at the core, we believe that for the privacy-minded individual, the technology war is lost. You can employ and even pay for many online services to preserve your privacy but, at the end of the day, if the opposition is strong enough, you are wasting your time and money. Worse yet, you may be laboring under a false sense of security that in the end can doom you. If we can state one single maxim to guide you through your quest for privacy and security, it is going to be this: *Less is more!*

The more mail you receive, the more people have your phone number, the more email you send, the more social media you are active in, the greater your footprint. And the greater the footprint, the more difficult it is to maintain your privacy. That said, there are things you can do to limit your exposure without having to give up everything you love. Of course, the need to take back some privacy or even to disappear varies from one situation to another. At the outset, you should, therefore, begin with an in-depth assessment of the opposition. Ask yourself what specifically you are running from and what is required in order to accomplish your goal. As we have stated previously, the challenges are different if you are dealing with family or personal issues or are the target of a government hunt.

The overwhelming majority of data on an individual is generated, consciously or not, by the individual herself. Every time you fill out an application, sign up for a service, open an online account, or create an online profile, you are giving out a lot of data that can be used, collated, and integrated by multiple commercial and government operators. All of that information can, at some point, be used against you. Even harmless-sounding services that you share your information with, or which can gain access to it indirectly, can use that information to manipulate you financially, to track you, or even to discriminate against you based on demographic analyses.

When sharing personal information, the most common misconception is that a person should share her personal information every time she is asked for it. In point of fact, in most instances, there is no legal requirement to provide information; and, if it comes to that, you can forego whatever benefit is offered to you and not provide the information that is being requested. There can be various scenarios in which we have to decide as to whether or not to give out our biographical information. If we are buying a book, for example, and pay cash for it, we are not sharing any information. But if we decide to use a credit card or customer loyalty card to buy the same book or are forced to do so by today's economy and buy it online, we may be requested to fork over lots of personal data. You should then ask yourself this. If it is not necessary to provide personal information when buying an item in person and for cash, what legal obligation should there be to provide accurate information to buy the same item online? It follows that taking defensive measures to avoid sharing personal data, in most cases, is not only legal but just. And we can opt out of those activities that legally force us to share information.

In many instances, we are verbally asked to fill out a personally intrusive form or to answer specific questions such as date of birth and address. You would be surprised by how many people comply with the request just out of politeness or because they believe it is the right thing to do. But for a privacy-minded person or someone in real need of anonymity, that mindset needs to change. Changing your attitude involves becoming a little more assertive vis-à-vis some of the people you interact with. Appearing self-assured goes a long way toward limiting the intrusive behavior of others. When confronted with personal questions that we do not wish to answer, there are easy ways to fend off those questions without being rude. For example, you can say: "I am in something like the witness protection program, so I cannot provide the information you are requesting." That response will shut up most people. And for those who persist, you can add: "Unfortunately, I have not been authorized to discuss this with you." That statement, incidentally, would technically be true, as no one has authorized you to discuss anything.

To maintain or regain privacy, it is also important to start thinking differently about the world around us. The idea that we have to follow the trend and give up our privacy because that is what everybody else does is nonsensical. To varying degrees, we should resist this kind of pressure. The more we avoid sharing information, the easier it is to live under the radar. It is not an easy task these days, but it can be done. And, as we have stated earlier, the main part of this form of resistance is not to fight but to avoid the onslaught of the digital revolution around us. As we have mentioned before, we are going to list the various items that can help us regain the lost privacy.

Your Name and Date of Birth

The name most people use is their birth name. But names can be changed for several reasons, so you should not think of your name as an inevitable and immutable characteristic. There are nicknames, new names, married names, screen names, and many other variations of what can identify a person. But more on that in the chapter on identities.

You should not rush to provide biographical information to any stranger who asks for it. If you are making a restaurant reservation, for example, there is no reason why the restaurant should have your biographical details. And if you fail to provide accurate details, there is no harm done as the restaurant is not *entitled* to get that information to begin with. The restaurant example is just one of a multitude of situations that you can encounter in your daily life where making the right decision can make the difference between cutting down your exposure or magnifying it.

Customer loyalty cards are an example of marketing where you *voluntarily* provide personal data in order to get a discount. But since anyone can get a discount card, it follows that the whole practice is a gimmick to get customers' information. And the information you provide, like your name and address, may be sold and resold until some day it may be used against you by someone. Just the notion that a major corporation knows your name, where you live, your age, and what you buy should be offensive to an ordinary person. Except that most people do not think that way. They assume that because they have nothing to hide, they should not be afraid to tell the world all about their personal life and data. But, as we will explain throughout the book, all of the personal data you have given away may come back to haunt you.

Your date of birth is a fundamental identifier, along with your name and photograph. Unless you are somehow managing to get a whole new identity, there is not much you can do about that. But, the point is to lower the number of places where your birth date is on file.

To make this simple: Stop giving out your name and date of birth unless it is necessary. Stop joining groups, clubs, online services, and all other forms of social and commercial interaction unless you use one or more nicknames. If you think about it, you can get away with it; and, in the long run, this practice will be worth your while. In unofficial situations, you may also consider "mistakenly" inverting digits or letters so as to confuse the picture.

Your National Social Security Number

Do not, repeat, do not give out your social security number unless it is legally mandatory and necessary and, even then, think about it. Your name, address, and social security number are all someone needs to steal your identity. When you visit a doctor and they ask you to fill out a form, you may notice that somewhere it asks you for your social security number. Now, what need does the doctor have for this information? None. And yet, the number may be passed on to insurance companies, hospitals, pharmacies or, God forbid, lawyers. But you can refuse to provide the number by just saying that you do not provide your social security number or don't have one to give. Surprisingly, life goes on, and you will have lived to fight another day.

ID Cards and Passports

Unless you are in a position to adopt a new identity, you are stuck with the ID or passport you have. But you don't always have to provide them when requested. In any event, it is far better to use a passport than a driver's license because at least the passport does not contain your address while the driver's license does. Unless of course you use a "safe" or "ghost" address on your driver license, in which case, you are on the right track.

Photographs

For the love of God, take down all of the pictures you have posted on the Internet–websites, social media, everything! And tell your friends not to post any of your pictures as you are going through marital problems or have a stalker looking for you or whatever. It is bad enough that your official photos, as per your driver's license and passport, are already in the possession of the government. The more pictures you add to those officially in government databases, the more you are adding to the ammunition of the opposition. If you are planning a clean exit from your current situation or location, it would be a good idea to also remove from your house pictures of yourself lying around or those in an album. "Mr. Wilson, can you tell us what this live-in girlfriend that robbed you looks like?" "Oh yes, officer, I even have pictures of her that we took on our trip to Barcelona. In fact, they should be right there on the dresser. Oh, wait a minute, they are gone!" Less is more!

Address

For someone looking for anonymity and/or safety, the home address is, or should be, the sum of all fears. Anybody can get your official address. The Department of Motor Vehicles; your employer; your doctor; your bank; your credit card companies; private investigators; the police; and anybody who is looking for you, friend or foe. Someone who means you harm can get your address of record in a heartbeat. Not only that, if you own the house where you live and that is your address of record, anyone suing or *contemplating* suing you will know that you own at least that asset. And that is one more reason to sue you even if the case has no merit. That is because many lawyers, officially or not, work on some kind of contingency and will not get involved if they do not see a pot of gold at the end of the rainbow–like your house, for example.

Before you panic, pause for a moment and think of what the word "address" means. An address can in fact mean different things. It can be a place where you receive mail, a designated place to receive service of a process, a vacation retreat, or a place where you spend a lot of time. It is nobody's business where you sleep or spend your private time. You have a right to live on a boat, with roommates, in a motel, in a motorhome, or just wander. So here is a major point to remember: If you need to protect yourself or your loved ones, listing your private, personal home on any official or unofficial document is a major vulnerability. You are exposing yourself whether you do it on your checks, on an insurance form, on your driver's license, or in a customer loyalty program. Without breaking any laws, it is safer to use a mailing address or any address other than where you physically live. If you are learning this for the first time, wait until you move, and then make your next address a secure one. Or move now if you are under threat.

As soon as you are ready to move, pick a different place, far from your actual new residence, and start receiving mail at that address. It could be an office (or suite) address, a friend's house, or even a P.O. Box. Some companies or agencies do not accept a P.O. Box number as an official address, but that is easily resolved. Since every post office has a street address, list that street address first, followed by the P.O. Box number. The address could be something like this: 126 Overbrook Road, Box 1245, Canberra, Australia. You will get all your mail with no one challenging the arrangement. As soon as you have received a few pieces of mail, bring those to wherever you are asked for a proof of address. Before long, every record on you will reflect the address you created. And you should be practicing mentally to recite the new address and blocking in your mind, if you can, the actual residence you are trying to protect. No one will get your residence address unless you give it to them yourself or they get it from official records, which normally use the information on file with the Department of Motor Vehicles (DMV). As previously discussed, if you are under surveillance and are being followed or your phone is being tracked, then they could get to you anyway, but you have to start somewhere.

The above strategy is straightforward, with some caveats. If you are renting the house where you live, there may be records created by the leasing company, especially if they check your credit. But that is limited. Once the lease is signed, their credit checks usually come to an end. If you are buying the property, things can get more complicated. The major challenge is the mortgage, which will inexorably tie you and your credit history to the address of the property you are buying. But there are ways to resolve that problem. First off, do not take out a mortgage. That may sound harsh, but protecting your privacy is only one of many reasons not to take out a mortgage. From a financial point of view, mortgages are a rip-off. If you look at the price you will be paying over the life of the loan, you will see that you are going to be paying several times the value of the loan and the property. Better to save and buy a cheaper house for cash. If you really need to borrow, you can try a personal loan *not* secured by or connected with the property. The purchase would then be a cash transaction where little information needs to be disclosed.

When it comes to taking title to a new residential property, never ever take it in your own name. If you did that, in one scoop, you would blow your privacy, and, at the same time, expose the asset to any would-be plaintiff. Remember that if your name shows no assets, that is the best insurance policy against lawsuits you can get. When you buy in cash, realtors and sellers are busy selling and getting your money. They couldn't care less what name the property is going to be titled in. They will do it exactly the way you want it. The situation is different when you sell because there may be issues of capital gains taxes, but that is not going to affect your future privacy.

There are several options when it comes to taking title to a property; and, on that, we refer you to the chapter on asset protection. For the purposes of protecting the privacy of your residence, we have to repeat that your name must never appear on a property search. Because a property search is one of the first steps a private investigator takes to locate you.

You should not receive any mail at your new residence. If you have taken title to the new property under the name of, say, ABC Ltd., then the only mail delivered to that address should be for the corporation. And the corporation, or better a trust, should not have your name anywhere near it. The mail for the corporation could also be sent somewhere else, like an office or P.O. Box. You will also need to be very careful with the utilities. If you are one of the few people who still use a phone landline, make sure the number is unlisted and not in your name. If you have a mobile phone, the bills, if not paid online through an anonymous account, should go to the address where you receive mail. For all other utilities, you need to be creative. Try to keep them in the name of the former resident of the house if possible and, if not, put them in the name of the corporation that owns the house or in the name of a friend. Whatever you do, your name and the new address should not be connected under any circumstance. If you receive mail or packages at that address, the address is blown. Insurance on the property may be your undoing, so try to self-insure, if you can. Insurance is usually a rip-off anyway, and it will connect you with the address. If you are taking out a mortgage, they may force you to keep insurance on the house, which is one more reason to avoid a mortgage.

In spite of all the above-mentioned precautions, if you are truly under threat, those precautions may not be enough. There are ways in which a determined pursuer could locate you. One is by physically following you, either on foot or by car. So, when you are approaching your house, take care to check if there are people or vehicles in your vicinity that do not belong there. In some cases, you may have to take a detour to be sure you are not being followed. Another threat is your mobile phone. The phone can provide your exact location, so make sure the phone is off before you approach your home; and, if you believe it may have been compromised, remove the battery. Unfortunately, some phones do not allow that; so, in extreme cases, you may need to shield it.

Cars and Other Vehicles

One of the deciding factors in choosing a new place to live if you are trying to disappear or lay low is whether your chosen location forces you to have a car. Details on those issues will be discussed in the chapter on destinations. To be clear, if you are striving for anonymity, this author discourages having a car or other vehicles in your name. As we noted earlier, any vehicle that requires registration, insurance, and plates is going to create huge exposure. But, assuming that you must have a car, there are ways to lower exposure. First of all, the address used for the registration and insurance should be the same as the one on your driver's license, which, as was explained above, may be your mailing address but should not be your physical, private residence. Remember that all databases, driver's license, insurance, and vehicle registration are interconnected. As long as everything matches, you are probably OK, but not completely. The reason for that is that someone following you home not only will get a pretty good idea of where you live, but they can also match the information they get from your license plate, which identifies you, and connects your car and mailing address. They will then be able to confirm that the mailing address you use belongs to you and whichever entities you have been using. And they will then be sure to check what other mail you receive at that address in addition to mail related to your vehicles. Like notices regarding your corporations, utilities, mobile phones, and much more. Nasty stuff!

One way to segregate your vehicles from both your private residential and your mailing address is to register the vehicle to an LLC, corporation, or trust that uses a different address; and for those details, we refer you to the section of this book on assets. But it is enough to understand here that a corporation or trust can own a car and can be domiciled anywhere. One caveat, however, is that the Department of Motor Vehicles can require information on the person driving the car, as will the insurance, and that would link you, the driver, with the separate address used for the corporation. You could also put the car in the name of a friend or relative. Tread carefully, however, because you could be dragging your friend or relative into your own predicament, whatever that is. Remember also that today's friend or lover could become tomorrow's enemy. The more you can accomplish on your own, the better.

Money

You may have heard the expression "cash is king." Nowhere is that more true than in the context of privacy. Most people understand the anonymity of cash. But we suggest that you make a habit of using cash as a way of life, whether or not any particular transaction requires anonymity. You will thus reduce your exposure in many ways. Any payment that you make using a bank check, a transfer, or a debit or credit card is going to be linked to you thoroughly and completely. It will show not only the particular transaction but also the pattern and location of your spending. It will stay on the books forever and can be accessed by law enforcement as well as private investigators. An exception can be made for prepaid debit cards, but that is an almost obsolete exception, as recent legislation to combat terrorism and money laundering usually requires registration of those cards. Of course, if you are in a position to register under an alternative identity, you might get the privacy you crave, but you may be breaking the law. Gift cards that you cannot reload can work without registration, but their use is limited. Money orders are far better than debit or credit cards. In theory, cash can also be traced due to serial numbers of notes and fingerprints left on the notes themselves, but you almost never have to worry about that unless you have just robbed a bank, an activity which, naturally, the author of this book would condemn.

Anonymous bank accounts are a thing of the past due to the same legislation that bans anonymous credit cards and for the same reasons: terrorism, money laundering, and tax evasion. Those regulations end up mostly affecting honest people that harm no one and break no laws. And that is one more reason to try and keep your transactions private.

The most popular offshore tax havens that advertise their efficiency and secrecy are the Bahamas, Panama, the Cayman Islands, Dominica, Nevis, Nauru, Gibraltar, Luxembourg, Switzerland, Vanuatu, and many others. In spite of what they tell you in their brochures, however, each and every one of them has signed agreements with countries in the European Union, the UK, the U.S., and other developed nations from where big money tends to come. Those agreements are called TIEAs, which stands for Tax Information Exchange Agreements. In essence, those agreements kill bank secrecy by opening the bank accounts to the scrutiny of tax collectors of wealthy nations. Exceptions might be Lebanon, the Philippines, and similar jurisdictions, but laws are in constant flux.

Another casualty of all the new laws and agreements are bearer bonds, which are certificates that allow any holder to take over a corporation, including its bank accounts. You then have other urban legends, such as Austrian "sparbuch" savings accounts that are supposed to be totally anonymous. They are advertised all over the Internet. But you probably can tell that something is wrong when they discuss Austrian shillings when that country has been using the euro since the year 2002. Watch out for those scams! In dealing remotely with any brokers or lawyers, just use the same common sense you would use at home. If they do not have a brick-and-mortar building address with a phone landline, just forget about them. The chances are, it's some criminal working off of her computer in China or wherever.

Does the fact that bank secrecy is mostly dead mean that you have lost all privacy protection for your savings? Not necessarily. For one thing, you should never ever open an offshore account in your own name. Any search performed officially or even illegally will turn up your name. Assets that you keep in the same tax haven would be found very quickly. But it would not be so easy if the account was opened in the name of, say, Dusty Rhodes, Ltd. With thousands of corporate accounts for every bank, it is very hard to narrow the field to find the assets one is looking for. Even if someone were able to focus on the account of Dusty Rhodes, Ltd., in the belief that you are the beneficial owner of the corporation; and, therefore, the account, they may find that that corporation is a wholly owned subsidiary of Skip Towne, Inc. of the Seychelles, a different jurisdiction with different laws and requirements to search accounts. Furthermore, certain jurisdictions only permit disclosure of banking information under limited circumstances. With every layer you add between you and the opposition, the job of locating your nest egg becomes more difficult.

The only catch to these privacy maneuvers is that, in theory, to open a bank account in most places, you are now required to provide a financial profile and ID of the person opening the account. But, of course, that person could be a lawyer, the same lawyer who set up one or more of your corporations. With a power of attorney, she would be acting as treasurer of the corporate entity and be in charge of accounts. But that arrangement need not last forever. The treasurer could at some point be replaced, like 5 minutes after opening the bank account, for example.

Another option for the creative individual in search of anonymity is the use of Bitcoin or other digital currencies. In some cases, that option can offer more transactional privacy, but there are some drawbacks. One of them is that digital currencies are often used by criminals and are, therefore, viewed with suspicion by law enforcement. That, in turn, can attract undue attention to your own perfectly legal operation. As always, the trick to staying out of trouble is to always follow local laws and those of your own country, to pay your taxes, to support your family, to support the community, and to live in peace. At least that is what the lawyers told us to write.

Store Discount Cards, Club Membership Cards, Organ Donor Cards

Cut up everything that you do not absolutely need and scatter the pieces to the wind. Remember that less is more!

Travel

We have covered the dangers of airline and other registered travel, and we will be going into strategic travel in the section on vanishing acts. We would, however, encourage healthy privacy habits at all times. If you want, for example, to visit certain locations without leaving big signs of your presence there, you must use common sense, but that may not be enough. For one thing, better to travel alone. If you take public transport, take a bus or a train that does not require advance reservations. Buy your ticket in cash. If they ask for a name, well, you can get creative, since your name is none of their business anyway. If you travel by car, try to buy fuel by paying in cash, at your point of departure. No need to leave traces along a journey you do not wish to advertise.

Internet

Our "less is more" philosophy has already been made clear. The Internet is a wild and dangerous place. It does offer many opportunities, especially for those who are building a new persona. But for someone in a delicate, transient situation, it can spell doom very quickly. In essence, you have to ask yourself: Do you really need to go online all the time? Can you accomplish the same things, like buying a gift, planning travel, reading a book, doing research, checking the weather, without going online? You will find that most of the time, the answer is yes. And if you do not really need to go online, don't. Because everywhere you go, every activity you undertake, every website you visit, you are leaving a signature. And your activity online can tell the story of your life–your plans, your worries, your dreams, your buying habits, your taste, your social life, and your family life. Someone auditing your browsing history is probably going to be able to predict your next moves. They will know not only where you've been but also where you are probably going. And that, gentle reader, is a bad place to be if you are on your way to the Land of the Disappeared.

That said, even online, there are things that you can do to minimize your exposure. One problem with browsing is that every website you visit tends to deploy cookies; and your activity and data are, therefore, stored, sold, and resold. That is annoying because you end up seeing all of those ads following you. But it's not only ads you need to worry about, it is also the broadcasting to the world (and probably to the opposition) your browsing history. A way to avoid or limit that is to disable cookies, and there are many simple ways to do that. Or you can use a more private browser, such as DuckDuckGo, that claims it does not track you; so you can take back some privacy that way.

A bigger problem, however, is the Internet provider (IP) address. An IP assigns an address to every user who logs into their network. That works like a phone number that connects to the millions of sites in the universe of the Internet. Think of it as a number tattooed on your arm. In order to be anonymous online, you, therefore, need to conceal the IP address. A popular free service, called Tor, allows you to surf the Internet by concealing your IP address. It can make your address look like it is accessing the web from a different or foreign location. The websites you connect to are not able to see your true location or what your browsing habits are. There are also virtual private networks, or VPNs, that charge user fees.

In addition to Internet provider exposure, most commercial email providers breach the privacy of your inbox. If you want more secure email addresses, you would do well to choose a smaller provider. Currently, among the best are the Swiss-based Proton Mail and Kolab Now, Netherlands-based StartMail, Swedish Countermail, the Norwegian Runbox, and Tuta Mail. Can you trust them? Maybe, until they get a subpoena from Big Brother to fork over all your stuff.

The software remedies mentioned above are very good in theory but, in reality, they are not foolproof. If you use any personal information on TOR or other network, like your personal email or a credit card, that will of course nail you. Javascript can also work to reveal your IP address and should, therefore, be disabled; as should some other features of your browser. There is also word out that governments track Tor users; and, therefore, using it increases rather than decreases the chances of exposure. Even if you are on top of the latest technology, your habits can give many clues as to where and even who you are. Discussing local sports or weather, or mentioning specific restaurants or local people can add pieces to the puzzle that ultimately can reveal your identity. But the main vulnerability of these technical solutions is that at some point you can trip, all while you enjoy a false sense of security. Better, in this author's opinion, to assume that your communications are *not* safe and work your way from there.

A low-tech approach to maintaining a certain degree of anonymity is to buy a laptop or gadget in cash without registering it or the software that comes with it. You can use it for occasional Internet browsing at free Wi-Fi spots as long as you never input any of your personal information like email addresses and do not register on any websites where you are otherwise known. The website will remember your device, as will the opposition, but they will not know your personal identity. That system can work, but there are limits. The pattern of local use, such as free Wi-Fi cafés, can say a lot about you. It can lead an investigator to guess the general location of your residence, office, or place you regularly frequent by triangulation analysis. Not to mention physical surveillance in cases where someone really wants to identify a certain user visiting sites on a given list. And then, of course, there are the ubiquitous CCTVs with digital imaging and practically unlimited storage.

Smart Phones

If you have read this far, you can probably guess that we do not recommend using your regular phone for sensitive conversations. A prepaid phone is the way to go. Use it once, and then ditch it; or, if money is really important to you, you may try to return it by complaining about the sound quality. One very popular app, called WhatsApp, allows people on the app to chat with one another on their phone for free and even exchange pictures and videos. It is now evolving into another social media platform. The communication itself is supposed to be encrypted at both ends, and that provides a modicum of privacy. But when you use your own phone to initiate the communication or partake in it, there will be a record of it. There have also been revelations from WikiLeaks that the U.S.'s NSA has cracked WhatsApp encryption systems.

There are on the market so-called secure phones that ensure privacy between people talking on those phones. One company that makes them is Silent Circle. As long as you are using such a phone to talk with someone in the same system, your communication is supposed to be secure. Or is it? Many questions linger in the mind of this author regarding such claims. First of all, if you buy such a phone, even if you use some form of prepaid and anonymous debit card, it will have to be shipped somewhere. And wouldn't you think that the government keeps an eye on purchasers of these devices? One also wonders who the creators of the software are and if any other parties have participated in the design. And where are these devices made? How are they shipped and by whom? Where are they stored, and who has access to the storage place? Who packages the items for shipment? How are employees of the companies involved vetted? There may be ways to test the security of these devices if an end user is also a computer expert. But, in general, our opinion is the following: It is better for two people who need a seriously private conversation to purchase burner phones. Talk away, and then ditch the items. The conversation will be random, like two ships passing in the night.

Laptops and Other Computers

Buying a computer may seem a straightforward process, but a few common sense measures must be taken. Since your computer will at some point contain your personal information or other identifiers, you should never buy it online and should never pay using a credit or debit card linked to you. Simply go to a store far away from your place of residence, pay in cash; and avoid any type of registration for the warranty, discount, or anything else. And once you boot it for the first time, avoid registering; and, if you have to, never use your name or address. There are many reasons for that. First of all, once you use a name in the registration, that name will show on the data of any document you create. And if the machine ever goes online, all of that information can be exposed. In fact, if you are planning to store sensitive data on the computer, do not ever go online with it, and make sure you disable any Wi-Fi or transmission mode. You can use a different device for online activities. But if you transfer data from the virgin computer to online, make sure data does not carry any identifiers.

Email Addresses

It is amazing how many services, purchases, and other activities are tied to your email address. It has become almost impossible to sign up for anything online without an email address. The problem with that is that, most of the time, the email address you use can link back to you. So if you are trying to be anonymous, that is a real problem. Any time you try to create a new email address, the system asks you for a backup address; and, of course, that would link back to you. If you use a friend's address, in a crisis and given enough pressure, your friend will give you away; or the opposition will audit her email correspondence until your information comes up. If you search online, you will find a lot of useless services that will sell you a way to mask your email and even your phone number. While that may work to avoid spam, it will do nothing for your anonymity. When push comes to shove, the online company will hand over your information so fast your head will spin. So that is a waste of time and money.

One of the best ways to get a truly anonymous email address is to start with the cash purchase of a prepaid phone; and sign up on Google, Hotmail, or other email provider using the new number as backup reference. As to your personal information necessary to register, you may decide to use all of your creative powers, since they should not be asking for your personal information to begin with. Once you have your first truly anonymous baseline, you can get other email addresses and even Zoom or similar services. But remember to never use any of those anonymous tools to call a number connected to you, write to an address connected to you, or sign up for anything that is in any way connected to you. Use your newfound freedom sparingly, and tread carefully. If you are using Zoom, make sure you do not do that from a device registered to you or using your IP.

Apps

Of all of the frauds and scams in contemporary society, many apps are very close to the top ranks. It used to be that if you wanted information or a service, you could go to a website, do your research, and maybe hire someone. You could also bookmark the site for easier access in the future. That is almost past history, as you are now asked to download apps. They sell these things as better than plain websites because of "use optimization." Even if that is sometimes true, there is a lot more that apps do once you download them than just make your life easier.

One thing that almost all apps do is to place cookies on your device. Those cookies are there to suck up your information, store it, and usually share it with third parties. In some cases, your data is needed for some functionality, but most of the time it is completely unrelated to the job of the app. For example, why would a travel site need your contacts list? Why would a translation service need your location? The answer is that that is where most of their profits come from. Just imagine a real-time auction of your data as soon as you open a site. And permanent little bugs in your computer to keep mining your data.

Apps do not necessarily simplify your life, and they can actually make it more difficult and expensive. Imagine, for example, that you need a job done in your kitchen that you are not able to perform yourself. In the good old days, you would go to someone that does carpentry or tile work, but not anymore. Now, you need to go online; and a search for carpenters will almost never yield names of craftsmen in the field. What you find is a list of companies that advertise kitchen remodeling. But those are not the craftsmen you are looking for. Those advertisers do not work on kitchens. They are inanimate software apps that want you to sign up for a service based on (you guessed it) your needs, your location, your budget, and many other things. Supposedly, if you sign up, you may be linked to companies that may be interested in doing the job you need. But even if you get there, after divulging tons of your personal data, you may be placed in touch with another layer of speculators who employ low-skilled workers at minimum wage, after paying a cut to the online app. And you will probably end up with a substandard job after paying the middle men and speculators with your money and your data.

This discussion is not to make a case for avoiding all website interactions and apps but to just ask yourself if you really need all of that stuff, or can make your life a little simpler and easier by eliminating clutter.

Physical Security

If you are contemplating an exit from your location or situation, or are well on your way, at some point you will need to consider who may be interested in "raining on your parade." What the opposition is going to look like is something only you can tell. But, sooner or later, you will be looking over your shoulder for unwelcome signs of interference with your plan. Are these people trying to talk to you? To serve you with legal papers? To transport you to a location where you do not wish to go? Or maybe to dispatch you to the next life?

If you are concerned for your safety, you should look carefully at people around you to determine who belongs there and who does not. But people who look familiar in one context are not necessarily a good omen if they are in the wrong place. If you are a Chinese dissident strolling on the streets of Paris and recognize someone from the Chinese security police, that is probably not a happy coincidence. In all cases where safety is involved, it is crucial to spot a tail and assess it. Sex, age, and fitness level are all important details, but also pay attention to what they are wearing, and we are not just talking about uniforms and fashion here. Loose garments, like a loose jacket, can be a problem because they can be used to conceal something, like a revolver, for example.

One key question you need to consider is whether or not to carry firearms. That would depend entirely on your situation, the kind of opposition you are facing, and the availability and legality of weapons in your area. There are several schools of thought on this topic. Some believe that you almost never need a gun; but, once you have it, you will be forced to use it, and that may place you at increased peril. The idea is that there are always going to be bigger guns out there, so you might as well give up. Others, on the other hand, think that it is better to have and not need than to need and not have.

The legality of gun ownership varies of course from place to place. One general rule if you live in a motorhome, perhaps of interest to some readers of this book, is that while you are driving, you are not allowed to have a loaded gun next to you. Essentially, it is the same rule as for cars where you are required to remove bullets from the gun, and store it in a separate place such as the trunk. In a motorhome, however, once you are parked and stationary–especially if you have chairs and other items outside–the vehicles becomes your legal residence; and you may, therefore, be allowed to carry a gun as you would in your house.

Those details notwithstanding, if your life is in danger, you may be tempted to go for safety rather than compliance. On this point, many gun owners insist that they would "rather be tried by twelve than carried by six." If, for whatever reason, firearms are not an option for you, you may consider carrying a knife or even a long screwdriver. Those would not have the same stopping power as a .45 piece but would be better than nothing in a confrontation. Pepper spray is a very common defense device and unlike tasers and stun guns does not usually require permits. Some people choose to just carry alarms or whistles. But let's face it, if you need to embarrass yourself with a whistle, you might as well give up and go down with dignity.

FOUR

IDENTITIES

The issue of identities is a complex one, fraught with legal uncertainty. What is legal and works in one jurisdiction may be illegal or problematic in another. In very general terms, the reasons for seeking a new identity can be a clue as to whether the process is permissible. For example, if one is attempting to commit fraud, just about anything she does to hide her identity should be considered illegal because it becomes part of the fraudulent scheme. But innocent use of nicknames for online activities is very common and usually legal, unless the online activity itself is illegal. Many women take the name of their spouse when they marry, a common practice that has been traditionally accepted. Performers frequently use stage names, and that has always been considered legal. In practice, however, performers will use their real names when signing contracts and other official documents.

Beyond these generalities lies a multitude of possibilities that should be considered on an individual basis. It should also be noted that laws can vary greatly from one place to the next and are often changed. The general trend, however, seems to be to restrict the use of new identities, which law enforcement likes to call aliases. One example is applications made to obtain credit. Using an alternative identity different from your birth identity to open a bank account or obtain credit is illegal in many countries, even though one may not be attempting to commit fraud. The reason for that is that a new identity, for credit purposes, could be treated differently from your old identity. When someone has a troubled credit history and would normally not be accorded credit, she might be able to obtain credit by using a new identity. And that logic may extend to the official use of one's name.

In today's society, as we noted earlier, one is constantly prompted to give out personal information. In some instances, there is an obligation to provide such information, but in the overwhelming majority of cases, there is not. If there is a legal obligation to give out personal details, one may assume that it is illegal to lie. Of course, if one's life is in danger, then it may be reasonable to withhold information or to lie about it, at least in part. In the context of online activities, it is common for most people to use a fake identity and even a fake or alternate email address. There are several online services that can generate anonymous email addresses and even phone numbers to avoid spam or unsolicited correspondence. It is important, however, to understand the limitations of such services. If you have signed up for such services using your credit card or have provided your personal information in any way, whatever new email address the companies give you can be traced back to you.

General discussions aside, there are several ways to change your name or identity, other than getting married and taking your spouse's name. Some are legal or closer to legality than others. This is, therefore, an area where consulting with a lawyer is advised.

1. In certain countries, if you use a new name for a long period of time that becomes your common law name. You just use it, and that's that. But legality is questionable if you have the new name inserted in official documents. That may depend on the laws or customs of the particular jurisdiction. In reality, in a world of digital information and terrorist threats, common law customs are dying out; and we are going toward universal records for all people. That's another reason to read this book. Multiple times, if necessary!

2. You can file an application with your local authority or court. In the application, you will have to state the reasons for the name change. An acceptable reason can be a safety concern. A woman who is being stalked, for example, might be better off using a new identity. Another example could be that of someone who has been given a name so ridiculous or inappropriate that she wants to change it. Another reason could be that one has been using a nickname, and she now wants to make that name official. The problem with the court procedure for the privacy-conscious individual is that it usually requires notice. Prior to the new name taking effect, you are usually required to post a notice or advertisement in a local publication, letting the world know that, going forward, you will be known by a new name. But such publicity may not work well for someone trying to become less visible if she fears harm.

3. In the old days, it was common for people who sought a new identity to adopt one from a deceased person. A short walk through a cemetery would provide a few names of people born around the same time as the person seeking a new identity. The preference would be for the name of someone who died as an infant. The reason for that is that as one grows up and lives an ordinary life, a lot of details are filled in, which may become problematic for the person adopting that identity. Once set on a new name and date of birth, someone could procure a birth certificate and then go to a Department of Motor Vehicles, Passport Office, or other agency and start applying for new ID documents. With a set of new documents, the new identity would then be set in stone. But that method of getting a new identity is now obsolete and in fact downright dangerous. The reason is simple. It used to be that agencies that kept track of births and deaths in many juris-dictions were not connected and did not, therefore, cross-reference data. In modern times, however, it is increasingly likely that birth and death records are computerized and cross-referenced. Applying for a driver's license in the name of a dead person would, therefore, raise some questions, at the very least.

4. In most countries, a person who acquires citizen-ship through naturalization is entitled to get a new name, and that becomes the official and only name for the new citizen. Or does it? It is hard to see how authorities can prevent someone from using docu-ments from the old country, which can probably be

renewed at the country's consulate. That would be true if the old country does not correctly receive the naturalization information and update its databases. Some countries ban dual nationality, but most do not or do not enforce the rule.

5. Obtaining a second citizenship practically without leaving home can entitle someone to also get a new name. Some people qualify for naturalization based on marriage to a citizen, long residency in a country, or employment-based sponsorship. For wealthy individuals and their families, there are also some countries that, essentially, sell passports. The list of countries that offer passports changes over time. Currently, the country of St. Kitts and Nevis offers two types of investment-based citizenship. One is through a contribution of a few hundred thousand dollars to the Sugar Industry Diversification Foundation (SIDF) and the other through the acquisition of pre-approved real estate. Dominica is another country that offers two types of investment citizenship. One is through a contribution to the Economic Diversification Fund (EDF) and the other through the purchase of pre-approved real estate. The country of Grenada also has a dual investment program: contribution to the National Transformation Fund (NTF) and pre-approved real estate purchases. These countries advertise their neutrality and stability and point out that with their passports, you can travel visa-free to many countries in the Caribbean and elsewhere. In this author's opinion, the citizenship offered by these countries is a useless waste of

money, even for citizens of countries whose passport poses challenges to travel. The reason is that most of these Caribbean nations are independent, and those who hold citizenship there are not allowed to work anywhere else or take advantage of the free medical system available in most developed countries (make that every developed country except the United States). It is not by chance that islands that are part of the United Kingdom or other European Union countries do not sell passports. Signing up for one of these investment programs, therefore, makes no sense. If you want to spend money, it is much better to try to acquire residency in a country of the European Union, such as Cyprus or Malta. Once a resident, and later citizen, of one of these countries, you will be able to work throughout the European Union and get free or almost free university education and medical care. The other problem of acquiring a new name through acquisition of a new nationality is that in order to enter countries such as the U.S. and others, one is required to either apply for a visa or provide fingerprints. And an application for a visa or providing fingerprints might reveal the old identity.

6. Rumor has it that some individuals who have run into extreme problems in their country have resorted to a diabolical scheme to create a new identity. It can work for those rare individuals who have never been fingerprinted and who do not have a picture on file with official authorities. A citizen of country X can file an application for asylum claim-

ing to be a persecuted citizen of country Z, a country with no diplomatic relations with country X and from where it is not possible or easy to obtain documents or verify information. By putting together a fictitious story of persecution in terrible country Z and employing a good attorney, some have been able to gain asylum and a work permit in country X. An approved asylum also comes with a picture ID and, based on that, a drivers' license, credit cards, and all of the documents that form the basis of a modern identity. Within a few years, the person accorded asylum can file for naturalization in country X and become, once again, a citizen of that country. New name, new life, and a new passport that could never be challenged, unless of course the fraud were exposed. What makes this scheme diabolical is that immigration laws are written to regulate the inflow of people, including asylum seekers. But, apparently, no one has thought about the possibility of someone trying to get citizenship in the country where she was born and of which she already holds citizenship. The author of this book of course does not encourage this scheme, as it involves lies and fraud.

7. By using the very technology that threatens privacy in the modern world, one can build an identity from scratch that includes all sorts of documents and even credit. If one has a credit card in her own name, for example, it is sometimes possible to apply for a second card with a different name. By using that card for purchases and other activities of contemporary life, the name used for the new credit card can

get a life of its own. The new identity can receive mail, promotional offers, and generate a whole new database. New credit cards could be obtained in the new name to make additional purchases and generate even more data. The drawback of this scheme is that, barring other arrangements, you can't use the new identity across borders. The other problem is that in a serious criminal investigation, a law enforcement agency can subpoena records from the credit card company and trace the identity back to the original credit card owner: you. That is, unless you have started from a fictitious baseline. Of course, this author cannot approve or recommend such endeavors if they involve fraud.

8. Have you ever wished you had been born in South America and were now a citizen of the place? If you have, your dream could become true. As this book is being written, a certain country in South America is going through a very tough economic period. There are food shortages, terrible inflation, high crime rates, and infrastructure trouble. In a period of crisis, however, some people become creative. And where some see a crisis, others see opportunity. According to our sources, a native of that country who needs to obtain or renew her passport encounters difficulties. The clerks at the passport office explain how expensive paper has become, how difficult it is to find the right ink and glue to put the booklet together, and many other difficulties. The problem, however, can quickly be resolved by paying a contribution of 500 U.S. dollars to the lifestyle of

the clerk processing the application. We are told, however, that these same clerks do not make the distinction between one who was actually born in that country and one who would like to have been. For the same contribution, and for a little more money, they can even expedite the issuance of the passport. It should be noted that we are talking about authentic documents. Once a citizen, always a citizen. If your passport is lost, stolen, or expires, you can renew it at any consulate in the world. And if the situation gets very bad in that country, who is to stop you from going back to your place of birth and applying for asylum? As long as your fingerprints are not on file, you can hit the ground running. But if you get caught, please don't tell them you've read this here. Especially, since we do not advocate this type of initiative.

9. The cheapest and most common ruse to get a new identity: false documents. False documents can be bought online or on the street and vary greatly in quality, from amateurish counterfeits to professional grade. In theory, such documents can help you cross a border. Aside from being illegal, however, counterfeit documents pose a serious danger to the user. There are basically two types of false documents. One is a stolen document in which the photo has been replaced. The obvious danger there is that a person from whom the document was stolen usually reports the theft. Border agents may, therefore, be on the lookout for a document bearing the name of the original owner or even the serial number. The

additional problem with that type of document is that the original owner may have been involved in a crime to which the new user may now be linked. The other type of false document is a genuine blank copy that was stolen from a government issuing facility or is created specifically from scratch. There, too, you have the risk of authorities using a database of stolen passport numbers or even checking the serial number against original issue documents. In addition to those problems, there is the difficulty of printing an ID document like a passport with all the embedded electronic chips and distinctive details that are now the norm in many countries. Adding to the worries of someone buying false documents is also the main question of whether you can trust someone selling counterfeit documents. How many copies of the same document have they sold? Has anyone been caught?

All the ruses described above involve attempts at getting a new identity or a double identity. But there are people who do not want any: They just play dead. Our advice is simply to not do it. There are so many ways authorities or private investigators can foil those plans that we won't even bother to make a list. Essentially, to fake a death without a body is virtually impossible, or at least not credible. And if you use another body that is supposed to be you, you are going to go down a very slippery slope. Where is the decoy body coming from? How did the person die? Hopefully, you did not cause the death. But even the most basic of forensic analyses will check fingerprints, dental records, and any other identifying details. They can then compare those with whatever is known of you, and the chances are that discrepancies will be found.

Most people pretend to be dead so that someone, usually their accomplice, can collect on life insurance. The trouble is that insurance companies will follow the beneficiary like hounds. They know that, at some point, somehow, the putative deceased will resurface and make contact. And that is when she will get nailed by the insurance with the help of police. These are serious crimes that should never be contemplated.

FIVE

ASSET PROTECTION AND ANONYMIZATION

The fact that you may be choosing to regain your privacy or start a new life does not mean that you should give up your assets. And that is true for several reasons. For one thing, there is no reason to part with something that belongs to you unless you want to. Secondly, you may find that in a transitional stage of your life and in new surroundings, you will need all of the money you can get. Last but not least, abandoning assets, like a bank account or a car, may actually help the opposition in locating you, and thus end your quest for freedom. This section of the book is not meant as a guide to asset management but focuses specifically on situations where privacy and anonymity are essential aspects of owing an asset.

The first order of business as you plan your move is to remove your name from as many assets that you own as possible. Bank accounts, real estate, automobiles, stock certificates, safety deposit boxes, and everything else connected to you must find a new owner. Preferably an entity that you control but a difficult one to find. You do not necessarily need to look offshore for this strategy, but that may be a forced choice if you have particular difficulties in the country you come from.

Of course, you could place your assets in someone else's name. But there are drawbacks to doing that, especially in the context of a vanishing act. You need the flexibility to access, transfer, or liquidate your possessions without having to wait for someone else to help. Even more important, the more information you share with others, the more exposure you will have. If you have a new identity, that would offer more possibilities, but most people do not have that option, or at least not until they have read this book. As to the traditional entities that are used for holding assets, we can summarize as follows: Partnerships will not help you. Corporations come in different types, mainly the regular corporation and the Limited Liability Company (LLC). The LLC is an extension of the person that owns it and can be easier to set up, with fewer requirements. Those corporations are very popular, but for the purposes of anonymity, there is no great benefit that this author can see. At least if corporate documents are searchable by the public, and that is the case in most jurisdictions. As explained below, new regulations on disclosure of beneficial ownership information, that is the person who owns the entity, will blow away the privacy of most structures you can think of. That is a very technical field and you would be well advised to seek the opinion of an attorney who specializes in privacy.

Another ownership vehicle is the trust, which comes in two main categories. The traditional, or irrevocable, trust is an instrument by which the settlor places certain property in trust for the benefit of beneficiaries and to be managed by a trustee. Once the conveyance is made, the settlor no longer controls the assets transferred. In the United States and some other countries, there is another form of trust called living, or revocable trust. That instrument is a combination of a trust and a will. It is mostly used to avoid probate, which is the complex and expensive process by which assets are distributed upon someone's death. The settlor places assets in the trust but can take them out or redraft the trust document until she dies or becomes incapacitated, at which point the trust becomes a will, or it becomes irrevocable in case of permanent incapacity. The primary reason for the choice of one instrument over another is tax planning and protection from lawsuits. While the author of this book recommends that you always pay your taxes, the focus of this analysis is mostly on flexibility and simplicity, so the choices may, therefore, be different than if you were trying to decrease your tax liability. Let's look at the various options in more detail.

A corporation is an instrument through which one or more people contribute money or assets and receive stock in exchange. A corporation needs an incorporator and also officers and directors. The corporation issues stock, which represents the value of the corporation. Holders of stock are called shareholders, and they vote to elect the directors who manage the corporation. In most cases, there are reporting and other requirements in addition to income tax returns that the corporation needs to file. The requirements vary from one jurisdiction to another. The more the requirements, the more complex the handling of the corporation. For a person on the move and under pressure to stay ahead of the opposition, the simpler the instrument and the lighter the requirements, the better. Ideally, you would want a requirement of only one director and one officer, who can be the same person and that could be you, your lawyer, or even another corporation.

Another instrument that is sometimes used to hold and protect assets is the international trust. Among the jurisdictions where those instruments are available are Belize,

Nevis, the Cook Islands, and the Isle of Man. Some of these jurisdictions are considered attractive because they do not recognize foreign judgments, or they make it difficult for a creditor to sue. Those trusts can be used in conjunction with offshore corporations to further insulate assets. Many offshore jurisdictions offer International Business Corporations (IBCs) with minimum regulatory requirements, ease of registration, and no taxation on income from foreign activities, that is all business transacted outside of the jurisdiction. These companies are ideal for holding assets, wherever those may be located. In selecting a jurisdiction to incorporate in, things to watch out for are the requirements for local directors, publicly accessible records of members and directors, and audit and account filing requirements. As you head for the Land of the Disappeared, you do not want any of those requirements.

Assets placed in the name of one of these companies are hard to track down, but not impossible. Somewhere, the name of the beneficial owner will appear, even if you set up several corporate layers in different jurisdictions. And on this issue, an analogy is appropriate.

If you think about theories on the beginning of the universe, you will notice that they all proceed backward from one event to another until they reach what is known as the "Big Bang," that is a mega explosion that scatters matter all over the universe. From all of those pieces of matter, planets, other objects, and galaxies emerge, and then solar systems, all the way to humans and our strange world. Those theories, however, do not convince this author, for one simple reason. What was there before the "Big Bang?" Whatever it was, it must have preceded the mega explosion, and that invalidates the origin theory. The world of offshore corporations can follow a similar pattern as an investigator tracks her way back from a known entity to corporate parents or affiliates in various parts of the globe. Following the corporate thread from tax haven to tax haven, she looks for the ultimate target: the owner or beneficial owner.

Given enough time and resources, a determined opposition will locate the owner of the assets, the head of the snake, if you will. But what if there is no owner at the end of the chain? That solution can be achieved by setting up what is known as a private interest foundation. You can set that up in Panama, Belize, and several other places. What makes a private interest foundation different, or very special you might say, is that it has no owners. The foundation owns the subsidiaries in the chain but is not itself a stock-issuing entity. Think of it as a nonprofit or NGO that pursues certain goals and is owned by the community. The only difference is that this entity is private and could not care less about the wishes of the community. Of course, it has officers and directors to manage it, but those are usually the lawyers that set it up. The only person that in effect has control is someone known as the "protector." The protector does not need to be listed anywhere, as she is not an officer or director. She simply "advises" the directors of her wishes. Obviously, care must be taken in making the payments to the lawyers in charge as well as in any communications. This is where the prepaid phones and Zoom-type services discussed above can come in handy. You could, of course, do all that in person, but there is one problem with that: your face. Someone at some point might remember you and, under sufficient pressure, might just kiss and tell. Better to send an "emissary," that is a local person met on the street, with instructions and documents. If you are in a tropical resort, your absence could be easily explained as a case of complications from a rum overdose.

What all the above-described instruments have in common is the need for a local incorporator or lawyer to form the entities and then maintain them. An entire industry exists in offshore locations, which serves wealthy foreigners and multinational corporations in search of tax avoidance or even evasion. In addition to the money needed to feed the army of offshore accountants, lawyers, and incorporators, there is the need for frequent communications. Such communications, whether by phone, email, or in person, create substantial exposure for the person in search of anonymity. They are in fact the weakest link in an attempt to disappear.

For the purpose of holding real estate such as the place where you live, or other assets, for that matter, an interesting option, and maybe the silver bullet, is the above-mentioned living trust. That instrument is only recognized in a few countries such as the United States. But the issue of being recognized or not has to do with taxation and probate and little else. So, if you need to set up an instrument that can operate as a will upon your death, you need to make sure that it conforms to local laws. If, on the other hand, you are only looking for an entity that can hold your properties and shield your name, then a living trust might do. A living trust is a beautiful thing. It is relatively easy to set up. In most places, there is no requirement to record it, and all you need to do to have official validity is sign it as the settlor in front of a notary public. The notary public does not read it and only sees the signature page. No copies of the instrument are kept anywhere, except in your head and in a drawer in your anonymous house or safety deposit box. You may even be able to draft the trust from a sample on the Internet and cut off the lawyers, the incorporators, the accountants, and all the other rip-off artists that inhabit offshore havens. One word of caution, however. If the trust was drafted on your computer, for anonymity purposes, it should be deleted. Unfortunately, deleted items can often be brought back to life by computer experts. It is better, therefore, to do the writing on a flash drive. Into the living trust, one can place not only real estate but also stock in a corporation that owns the real estate. For example, the trust can list stock in ABC Corp., which happens to own the house where you live. You would thus be adding another layer to the ownership structure.

Let's say that you have purchased a cabin in cash and placed it in the name of the Dusty Rhodes Living Trust. That trust is not recorded anywhere. It does not even need to have an address because you can make arrangements with the seller or title company to pick up the deed in person. The council or real estate taxes can be paid in cash or money order, as can the utilities, unless you are entirely off the grid, in which case there are no utilities to pay. You can even remove the mailbox if there is one. If the opposition wanted to find the owner of the property, they could do a property search and all they would find is the Dusty Rhodes Living Trust, no address of record, no incorporation, no recording anywhere. And if the property is in the name of a privately held corporation, whose stock is owned by the trust, the search may end at the corporate level without even reaching the trust. The opposition could search the whole world and never find the beneficiary of the trust. Conversely, if they looked up your name for an address or ownership record, the property would never come up, nor any reference to the trust. All this without paying any registration fees, maintenance, franchise taxes, or dealing with third parties. As we like to say, less is more.

GD Applegate

A word of caution at this point is necessary. Many countries have enacted or are in the process of enacting legislation that limits the right of privacy of corporate owners and investors. This recent regulatory framework mandates the disclosure of the "beneficial owner" of certain entities. Essentially, the beneficial owner is the main individual who owns, manages, or controls a given entity. Not all entities fall under these regulations but most do. In light of these recent regulations, the anonymity of the legal instruments described above must, therefore, be analyzed and updated in the applicable jurisdiction. Where there are reporting requirements, it is going to be difficult or illegal to hide the names of the beneficial owners. The choice of a country to base one's residency or assets is, therefore, also going to be based on the latest reporting rules.

SIX

DESTINATIONS

1. Town and Country

I f you ask ordinary people where they would go if they had to run and hide, inevitably you will get two separate solutions. Some believe that it is possible to escape from anything and anyone if only you can get far enough into a remote wilderness. The other camp, however, will point out that in a remote area where you do not belong, you will stick out more and will eventually be found. Easier, they will say, to disappear in a large city where you blend in and will be hard to spot. They are both right and wrong. Here's why.

Heading for a remote area has many advantages. For one thing, you can get a lot of distance between you and the opposition. You can find places with minimal population and a small likelihood of running into people you know or government authorities. Forests, wilderness areas, and the like can make excellent hiding places. But there are some major drawbacks. The main problem is that survival, let alone comfort, is next to impossible without goods and services unless you are entirely off the grid. Food, fuel, medicines, and many other items are hard to come by in the wilderness. Even if you can manage to hunt and fish and put up your own shelter, an infected foot could mean the end of your journey into the Land of the Disappeared, or this world, for that matter. Another big problem would be transportation. How would you get to the wilderness and carry all your stuff? And how would you get around once you are there? We have discussed in an earlier chapter the many dangers of owning and operating a motor vehicle. Registration, insurance, inspections, and plates are all document intensive. You can take a chance in not registering your car, but the first encounter with the law could doom you. Remember that where there are few inhabitants, there are also fewer patrols, but there are some. A lone driver without plates or an unkempt appearance would immediately attract attention. Getting fuel could also be a challenge, not to mention the need for a mechanic or auto parts.

Swampy areas, such as are found in parts of America like Florida and Louisiana, on the surface appear so remote and forbidding that few would go to look for someone in hiding. Those swamps are impressive in the movies and can indeed provide privacy. But they are also a hostile environment for all but a few hardy individuals. They tend to get lots of rain, and yet the soil is seldom adequate for agriculture and sustenance. Mosquitoes and other insects can be a constant nuisance as well as a health threat. Reptiles are often present in those areas, and they make wading in the water a bit dicey.

Canada's Northwest Territories, Alaska in the U.S., and the far north of Scandinavia also appear impressive wilderness areas where one could easily find refuge, away from crowds and the opposition. But, again, while those locations look good in movies, in practice, they are a very hostile environment. The climate is very harsh, except for a few summer months. The cold in the winter and even in the shoulder seasons is so intense that every aspect of normal life becomes difficult. During the long winters, even bare survival can become a challenge. Just to keep a small cabin warm and the pipes from freezing, assuming you have a working well, you need large amounts of fuel. Food will of course not grow, so you must stock up on it. Running out of food in the middle of a storm could be life-threatening. Transportation can be a problem, even with a four-wheel-drive vehicle. All that, without even mentioning the fact that work would be next to impossible to find. Social interactions, which in the long term are important, can be nonexistent in remote places. Deserts and other barren areas are also a bad idea for seeking shelter, for some of the reasons mentioned above. Extreme heat can also make certain locations uninhabitable.

A large city, especially a multi-ethnic metropolis, can be a great place to hide in. In a city, it is easy to find employment and other activities. It is also possible to get around without a car. But, there too, the challenges are many. A major threat are the ubiquitous CCTVs, controlled by both private entities and government. Then there is the cost of living, particularly housing. Purchasing a property in an expensive city would take time and likely involve documentation and a lot of money. Any large money transfer can trigger government scrutiny. Since most housing in cities consists of apartments, you would also be dealing with condominium or cooperative boards and regulations. Renting could also be a challenge as most landlords require references and a rental history. Most of the time, they will also run your credit. And for someone looking for anonymity, all of those formalities are deal breakers. Initially, one could rent a room from an Internet ad, but that would entail loss of privacy and inconvenience. A roommate situation would also invite many conversations and questions, and that is never good for those seeking total privacy. New friendships, for someone on the move and under pressure, are not a priority, to say the least.

In our view, a compromise location is the best approach. Avoiding mega cities, while not ending up in areas that are too remote, may be the right choice. A small town, or better yet, the edge of a small town, can provide the basic necessities while at the same time give enough space to maintain your privacy. On the outskirts of a small town, you might be able to find a cabin or hut that you can buy in cash and follow our suggestions on asset anonymization to avoid creating public records of ownership in your name. If you need to rebuild or fix the cabin you purchase, that is not a big problem, provided you are handy enough not to have to rely on too much outside help. What is essential, however, is that the infrastructure already be there (unless you plan to live entirely off the grid). If you need to build from scratch or redo major jobs such as connecting to a sewer system or electric grid, that will require lots of money and permits. And the permitting process is in itself a document-intensive activity that could easily expose your identity. In addition to obtaining permits, a major reconstruction project would also involve inspections, that is visits from officials from whatever authority is in charge of building activities in the area. Official visitors, however, may be the last thing you need.

Life in a small town can be simple. You may not need to own and operate a car. You can ride a bicycle or an electric bike. In most places, those vehicles are not regulated, which means no registration, no plates, and no need to carry a driver's license. You can also do some walking, which is both healthy and far more anonymous than operating any registered vehicle, be it a car or motorcycle.

One major issue in the selection of a place in the Land of the Disappeared is the weather. You most definitely want to opt for a temperate location. Extreme cold, with snow and ice, or a tropical setting subject to monsoons and hurricanes make daily life more difficult, not only from a quality of life standpoint, but also for anonymity. That is so because extreme weather can prevent you from walking, riding a bike, and fixing up your cabin if that is necessary. Extreme weather also makes it much more likely that you will need services; and, therefore, increase your interactions with the community at a time when you may not yet be ready for your social debut.

2. At Home and Abroad

One of the main questions for a person trying to disappear is whether to stay local or head overseas. There is no easy answer there because of all of the variations that one situation can present over another. It is also important to consider where the starting point is. Any location that is part of a large landmass offers many more possibilities than a small island nation. And the techniques for getting away can also vary greatly, but more on that in the chapter on vanishing acts.

The main advantage of heading overseas is the novelty of the area and surroundings. While a new environment requires some adjustment, the likelihood of running into known people, or the opposition, is much lower. In the event that there is an arrest warrant from the country of origin (of course we hope this does not apply to our law-abiding readers), the enforcement of that warrant is going to require an extradition request, which, at least in political cases, can be hard to obtain. Some fugitives also opt to go to countries that have no extradition with their country of origin or the jurisdiction issuing the warrant. Sometimes a little research can go a long way.

An additional benefit of moving overseas is that you can often break the chain of all of the old affiliations from purchase records to doctors, memberships in clubs and gyms, and all of the other things that form your personal profile in a given area. Assuming that you are starting out from a brand-new baseline and have severed all connections with your former self, a new country can be a great opportunity to start rebuilding your life from scratch. But you should be prudent and always avoid posting pictures on the Internet. We live in an interconnected world, and the Internet (as we have seen in an earlier chapter) can pose major threats to the person seeking anonymity.

The drawbacks of moving across borders, however, are many. Of course, at least in theory, you need travel documents to cross borders. Just applying for, or renewing, travel documents generates a lot of data on you. Someone watching your movements will get some important clues from the fact that you are applying for a passport. An application for a visa to go somewhere specific would blow a big hole in your anonymous trip, unless it is just a red herring you are planting to confuse the opposition.

In many border crossings, you will be going through customs and immigration. Customs officials have almost unlimited power to search you and all of your electronic devices. They can confiscate anything, download your files from computers and phones, and do just about anything else they see fit. Any right to privacy that you have in your home country is lost when you cross the border. By crossing a border, you are essentially granting the government much more power over you than they would have if you stay put. If authorities are on the lookout for you at the border, you can expect a major search. They will be looking at everything on your person and your bags; and, therefore, anything you have with you that you should not be carrying can be a liability. Like a copy of this book with a certain destination highlighted, for example.

Once a person arrives in a new country, she will be a foreigner and will not enjoy all the rights, including the right to privacy, that she enjoys at home. That will place her in a more delicate position, especially if her ID documents are a little bit tentative or only "temporary." An alien can encounter many limitations in her new country and is very vulnerable when the law comes a-knocking. There is always the possibility of deportation and even formal extradition if the opposition happens to be a major government with the right to grant, or withhold, aid money. If you are in that position, your arguments for the protection of your rights are likely to fall on deaf ears. Unless of course you are willing and able to pay off whoever happens to stop or detain you. On that point, it should be noted that an important part of a sensible disappearance plan should be a budget for, let's say, discretionary expenses. On a positive note for the privacy seeker, it can be said that in certain countries, one can find opportunities that do not exist in most developed nations. If you have a sizable enough budget, not only can you resist attempts by the opposition to execute warrants in your new location, but you can also actually make financial arrangements for your protection and security. At least until the money runs out.

The above discussion is only a general introduction to specific destination choices. Many factors need to be considered in specific cases. Your look, your age, your financial circumstances, and the reasons for your relocation all play an essential part in deciding where to go and how. Let's say, for

GD Applegate

example, that you are a black female in your thirties on the run. Naturally, this author recommends that you immediately turn yourself in but, for the sake of argument, we can examine your circumstances. Maybe you have left a messy crime scene and scattered your DNA all over your bed and the wall after you separated your husband from his male organ. You also forgot your framed picture on the nightstand and, because of that, your picture is now in all major newspapers under the title "Cut and Run" as well as on TV. Backpacking and hitchhiking in the Australian Outback in your situation may be a bad plan. It would be more sensible to head for the next big city and hope to blend in with the rest of the population.

3. Ideal Locations

The list of destination possibilities is endless, but any good relocation plan will take into account the pros and cons of every potential new place. Before we go into possibilities and suggestions, we need to emphasize the importance of your point of origin and the type of opposition you may be facing. Whether or not you have time to carefully plan your exit is another important issue to be considered. There may be ideal destinations that are not quickly reachable or not even suitable to those traveling in a hurry. Sometimes, a destination can be temporary with a view to moving on to some better or more permanent place at a later time. In order to stay ahead of the opposition, it may also be necessary to go, or pretend to go, somewhere that is not the true intended destination. The list provided below is not a simple discussion of retirement places but a general analysis of destinations for the person seeking anonymity and safety. And, if the place turns out to be pleasant, so much the better–fewer adjustment pains and fewer regrets!

Unfortunately for those fantasizing about an escape or those actually on the run, it is getting increasingly harder to evade the modern communication and transportation grid. In part, because of the temptations these technologies present. Wi-Fi is everywhere. Cellphone coverage is constantly expanding. From earlier chapters in this book, you have hopefully learned that a cellphone is a dangerous thing that can pinpoint your location to within feet of where you stand. And even where cellphone coverage is absent, you can use a satellite phone. But we hope you don't because, for the anonymity seeker, satellite communication is one hell of a bad habit. The analysis in this chapter is, therefore, not just about places to go but about avoidance of activities that can betray your itinerary to the opposition.

We can't possibly mention and rate all regions of the world as destination possibilities. But we can make a brief mention of the main areas that are often in people's imagination. And we also need to debunk some myths. So we begin with those choices that we think are in fact not so good.

Countries that are not completely independent or have not been universally recognized would seem to offer some advantages. South Ossetia, Abkhazia, and Transnistria are examples of those countries. Because the nations are not fully recognized, they usually do not have diplomatic relations and, therefore, no extradition treaties. You may also find more flexibility in mundane things, such as getting a local ID. And yet, barring special circumstances, your existence in any of these countries would be marginal and probably temporary. Since you are clearly not going to belong there, at any moment, you could be pushed out. If the country having real influence or formal jurisdiction over the region you inhabit really wants you, they can probably get you.

Remote areas in Australia are not even anywhere near the top of our destination list. In addition to climate and terrain shortcomings, there is the problem of getting there. That is unless you are already in Australia or have a friend with a Gulfstream jet who doesn't mind giving you a ride without adding you to the crew or passenger manifest. The same goes for New Zealand, a very pretty place where one can dream to be forgotten. But if you go there by commercial air, we can absolutely guarantee that you will not be forgotten and in fact will be nailed so fast your head will spin. Getting there by sailboat, on the other hand, will take a very long time from just about anywhere. And if it is not your boat you are traveling on, you will be adding several intermediaries to your adventure that could doom your anonymity.

China is said to be a popular destination for people who want to get away from the West and make a basic living by teaching English or other subjects in demand. But you would be rather confined there, and the authoritarian government would totally control you. In a police state, you might be safe as local things go, and may be beyond the reach of another government looking for you. But don't count on it. In the case of China, as in other totalitarian states, if it is in the political interest of the government to hand you over to whoever is looking for you, they will do it and will do it fast.

Southeast Asia has some terrific islands full of mystery and exotic things. We would like to specifically mention the Philippines, Thailand, Vietnam, and Cambodia. The eastern part of the Philippines, for example, is an area of great beauty and so remote that few tourists go there, especially in the small islands. The problem is, however, that like Australia and New Zealand, it is very difficult to get there. And not only that, it is also hard to get out. In addition to the out-of-the-way location, there is the issue of blending in. Unless you are Asian and of the local Asian variety, you will stick out like a sore thumb. And you must also consider the climate. A major monsoon will literally flush you out. And how would you get back to, say, Europe or wherever you are coming from, if you need to go back?

The European Union and the UK are not ideal places to run to if you are trying to disappear. These countries have long been fond of ID documents. With the wave of terrorism, things have become even worse. From labor to health care to every aspect of daily life, there is the omnipresent hand of the government. That may work for most people, but not for those wishing to disappear. Unless you are already in the EU and have a right to live there, that would not be on our list of easiest destinations. There are some exceptions. The canals of northern Europe, for example, are home to many canal boats that serve as a residence for many people, rich and poor. The rules seem to be less rigid for boaters, including liveaboards, than for the rest of the population. Still, even living on a pretty boat in a quiet canal, you are going to need services and interaction, which may prove difficult if you are not a full resident.

South of the Mediterranean things are different but not necessarily better. The Arab world of North Africa and the Middle East is plagued by conflicts and violence. Someone might have a particular reason or connections that would make a move there reasonable, but most other people would not make that choice. Morocco is somewhat of an exception, at least for tourists and those buying second homes. The country does indeed hold a magical appeal. From the central deserts to the Mediterranean and Atlantic coasts, there are myriad centers of art and culture. Tangier, in the north and a channel away from Gibraltar and Europe, in the forties and fifties used to have special international status and was a center of international intrigue. Writers, artists, spies, fugitives, adventurers, refugees, and many others used to congregate there and gave the city a very special character. On the Atlantic coast, Casablanca also had special status for a while and played host to many characters that one can describe, euphemistically, as eccentric.

Most of the atmosphere of intrigue and adventure has long gone from Morocco. Even though the country remains a good choice to get away from it all, bear in mind that it is ruled with an iron fist by a king who is a great friend of the West, especially America. If some government or powerful entity wanted to get you, your journey to the Land of the Disappeared could get cut off very quickly. There is a contested area to the south of Morocco known as Spanish Sahara. That area is coming more and more under the influence and control of Morocco, and any political statements in disagreement with that policy will quickly get a visitor on a plane out of the country. If you make it south of the border, you will then come under the jurisdiction of the Polisario Front, a political and military entity recognized by some governments but not others. If and how you would be received there is anybody's guess. But if you decide to go there, make sure to bring your camel and lots of water as most of the terrain is a forbidding desert.

Off the west coast of Morocco lie the Canary Islands, an archipelago that belongs to Spain, and hence the European Union. Nature is rugged and beautiful and the country is full of European tourists and residents, with a sprinkle of Latin Americans and Moroccan immigrants. Unlike Caribbean islands, it is possible to get there by ferry from the Spanish mainland. Some documents are required, but you would not fall under the information dragnet that an airline flight would trigger. And since the islands are so close to Morocco, it should not be difficult to hitch a ride on a boat going from there, or chartering your own passage on a Moroccan fishing boat. Once there, you will find a very civilized place with modern infrastructure and very low crime. You will also find, however, many of the same regulations and documentation requirements of the EU, but a bit more relaxed and informal. Connections to locals can go a long way to overcome those formalities. The Canaries are also one of the last places on earth where you will find few North Americans. So if you are experiencing problems in North America, this might just be the optimal destination in the Land of the Disappeared.

Canada is another highly regulated country, but the rigidity of the system is somewhat mitigated by the enormous size of the territory, which means a low population density. More open space also means less interaction with the organs of the state, including law enforcement. Barring special circumstances, however, for climatic reasons alone we would rate most of the country low on our list.

Caribbean islands, high on a list of tourist destinations, rank low, in our opinion, as a Land of the Disappeared. Small islands do not make for a good haven. Except by boat, to get to most of these islands you need to fly, which is not an option for those seeking anonymity. There is usually not enough room to move around. People remember an outsider. In case of trouble with the natives, there is no place to go. An exception might be Cuba. It is a large island and has long had inimical relations with the United States and cool relations with other Western countries. The island nation, however, is still somewhat of a police state. That means that foreigners can be tolerated but only as long as it suits the political establishment. But if you become *persona non grata,* you will feel the heat very quickly. As this book goes to press, the economic situation in Cuba is on a downward spiral. There is a strong possibility that some form of coup could take place with little warning. Who knows how a new regime imposed from Miami might affect your new life in the tropics?

Contrary to popular belief, the United States can actually be a pretty good bet for people flying below the radar. The enormity and diversity of the country, along with a culture of self-reliance and independence, make that country a fugitive's dream, if we may say so. Large immigrant and illegal populations, ethnic diversity, and a transient type of society make strangers of all kinds feel at home. In a sense, everyone is a stranger. What in other countries may seem odd, like living in a hut in the wilderness or in a trailer off the grid, in America can be normal. America is a place of contrasts, of creative people and eccentrics, billionaires and paupers, of wide spaces and freedom.

The great cities of America such as New York, Chicago, Boston, San Francisco, and others can offer a sort of shelter in that they are ethnically diverse and open to strangers and transients. The costs, however, tend to be high. And traditional housing rentals are often managed by companies and landlords that require credit checks and a rental history. These practices are problematic for someone who is trying to start fresh or is still on the move.

The further you get away from the densely populated East, the more people seem to have an independent spirit. In states like Alaska, New Mexico, and other places in the lower 48, there are entire communities who live off the grid. They live in buses and trailers, grow their own food, homeschool their children, and keep away from government and regulations as much as possible. All this does not seem to work too well for the socio-economic system. The disparity between the rich and the poor is huge and growing, and political education and participation are abysmal. But from the point of view of someone looking for another "roll of the dice," what could be better than Las Vegas?

In popular imagination, South America has long been the ultimate destination for people escaping from Europe and other developed countries. One of the advantages of South America is that, with the exception of the Darien Gap, it is drivable from Canada and the U.S.; and if you fly in from Europe or Asia to one location in South America, you can then take buses for long distances without producing any ID. And that would more or less beat the huge problem that flying presents for the anonymous traveler. In modern times, however, these countries have enacted legislation to regulate immigration. Most of these countries also have extradition treaties with European nations and America. They are in fact especially eager to please the U.S. and will bend over backward to ship back anyone of interest to Uncle Sam. Not only will they repatriate gringos, but they have often sent their own citizens to face American justice. For foreign travelers, they now require passports and visas, proof of income, and all of the other trappings of contemporary international travel. There are certain exceptions to this rule; but, in order to protect the innocent, we cannot say more.

Among large cities in South America, we would rate Buenos Aires very high for those seeking anonymity. With over 12 million inhabitants and comprising many different ethnicities, it is easy to see how one can blend in and disappear. The costs are somehow contained, and the quality of life is considered superb by many. Art, music, cuisine, and a laid-back attitude make the place a nice relocation option. There too, of course, you will find regulations; but in keeping with the general Latin character, arrangements can often be made to accommodate a wealthy person in difficulty.

If what you seek is wilderness, there is plenty of it in South America. Brazil, of course, has the largest rain forest in the world, the Amazon, that in places is completely remote and wild. The state of Pará is mostly lawless with unregulated mining, illegal logging, and slavery. But while lawlessness can bring a measure of freedom and flexibility to those seeking anonymity, the risks are just too great for most people.

The southern parts of Chile can be magnificent for the nature lover. Magallanes is Chile's southernmost region and one of the least inhabited. Araucanía is one of Chile's poorest regions and home to many Mapuches, a native tribe. The weather is harsh and difficult for normal life, especially for a foreigner. Among native populations, people from other countries will clearly stand out, and blending in is highly improbable. For all those reasons and the climate issues mentioned above, the wilds of Chile would probably not make for a good choice in the Land of the Disappeared. The populated, urban areas of the north would instead present the same challenges that you find in developed rich countries but with a little more flexibility.

On the border with Brazil is Guyana, an easy-going and user-friendly place with precious few tourists. In language, customs, and even political framework, the coastline is an extension of the Caribbean. The southern part of that country, however, is made out of one of the largest and unspoiled rain forests in Latin America. Some parts of those rain forests are almost inaccessible by humans. In the southwest is a huge desert savannah. The interior consists mostly of mountains that gradually rise to the Brazilian border. The highest mountain in Guyana, Mount Roraima, part of the Pakaraima's range, is on the Brazil-Guyana-Venezuela tripoint border. So you have extreme remoteness and three borders. Are you paying attention here? Remember, you are not reading an article in *National Geographic*. This is about disappearing, and this area is as good as it gets. But, of course, some of the comforts of home may be lacking.

Other countries in Latin America worthy of mention for the purposes of this book are Paraguay, which is a tax haven with easy residency for wealthy people, and Colombia. Paraguay, we think, is a little overrated as a destination of last resort. Of course, the Nazis found refuge there, but that was a long time ago, and things have changed. Colombia is delightful and a highly desirable destination–nice interior, Caribbean coast, and reasonable people. However, they have had a long civil war and a history of drug trafficking. Police and military are, therefore, very much on the scene and very friendly to the U.S. People with American trouble, therefore, should think twice before moving to Colombia.

Central American countries are very interesting for those dreaming of the Land of the Disappeared, but not all of them were created equal. Panama is a good place, especially for those seeking a tax haven and business opportunities. The ties with the U.S. and other large economies are so strong, however, that in such a small country, one can feel a little bit cramped. Costa Rica is another delightful little nation–no army, peace, social order, and many national parks. There are also huge numbers of expatriates and tourists. They have a universal health care system and other social safety nets. There are, however, large numbers of police on the beat and on patrol. It is clear that they are there to protect tourists and citizens alike. One wonders if the place is too regulated for those who prefer a truly anonymous lifestyle.

Nicaragua is one of the poorest countries in the hemisphere. A relatively soft land border used to get you easily into the country. But things are more rigid these days and the conflict between the current government and right-wing forces allied with their American patrons creates a lot of tension for residents and visitors alike. Foreigners can be viewed with suspicion and, in cases, even detained. The verdict on Nicaragua as a place of refuge is, therefore, a mixed one; and, in the end, the choice is up to the individual and her circumstances.

Still in Central America, we come to the finalists: Belize and Honduras. Belize is a favorite destination for expatriates–an English-speaking country at the crossroads of Central America and the Caribbean. You can visit the jungle in the morning and the beach in the afternoon. The place is peaceful, and it has a nice vibe with lots of ecotourists and environmental initiatives. You can get there by boat from Honduras and Guatemala and by road from Guatemala and Mexico. Entering from Mexico, near Chetumal, you can feel the general attitude of authorities. They try hard to look professional and make a big deal of stamping passports and asking routine questions. But you can sense that a few hundred yards from the checkpoint, the border is all wide open. And you could come in on your own boat all day long. Yet, the country is a transit point for drugs to North America, and that generates a certain amount of law enforcement and customs controls. That fact, along with the heavy tourist traffic, makes the place a little crowded and too close for comfort.

Honduras is a beautiful country plagued by poverty and gang violence. It is bordered to the west by Guatemala, to the southwest by El Salvador, and to the southeast by Nicaragua. It is on the Pacific Ocean and the Caribbean Sea. Most of the tourist action is on the Caribbean side and particularly around the Bay Islands, but tourism is also growing in other areas. Of particular interest to our readers could be La Mosquitia, the easternmost part of mainland Honduras, along the Mosquito Coast. It is a region of tropical rain forest and marsh, accessible primarily by water and air. La Mosquitia has the largest wilderness area in Central America, consisting of mangrove swamps, lagoons, rivers, savannas, and tropical rain forests. The lush jungle rain forest could be attractive for eco-tourists, but limited facilities and transportation make it a challenge for most travelers. And that creates an advantage for the person in search of peace and anonymity. Due to drug smuggling, the northwestern part of this region has a number of Honduran military posts and a base of the U.S. Drug Enforcement Agency, a rough bunch to get tangled with. Those looking for true anonymity would do well to avoid that area entirely. To the far east, however, lies a remote and, some say, forbidding part of the country. That is where you drop off of the "Gringo Trail" and go native. The local tribes of those parts are known to be a proud and loyal people. They could be ideal allies and protectors if that is where you had to make your last stand against the opposition.

SEVEN

OFF THE GRID IN STYLE

The idea of living off the grid is something that many people think about; but, in the end, few go through the trouble of actually giving up modern conveniences. We could detail many ways in which you can hide and survive while on the run. Camping is the most common way to do it. If you are in good health and know how to fish and hunt, you can set up camp in any area with a mild climate where nature abounds and humans do not. You regularly move and live a basic rustic life off public land. But it is a hard life that tends to not last for too long. Either you burn out, get sick, or just tire of living a life of deprivations and pain. There are better ways to go natural and still enjoy life.

Living off the grid does not necessarily mean giving up all comfort, and you can do it in style. You can, in fact, save money while enjoying a healthy life and contributing to a more sustainable planet. In addition to that, living off the grid the way we recommend can also help you take back your privacy. Keep in mind, however, that creating a truly off-the-grid retreat can be a multi-year project, and it requires some money, preferably cash.

It all starts with a piece of land that you own free and clear but not in your name. Ideally, it should be a beautiful place, a place with which you connect. This point is important because a speculative venture or mere investment does not give enough of a stimulus to carry out the many chores that are required to live off the grid. If you like mountains, by all means get a mountain lot as long as it does not get too much snow. If a beach is what you are after, then head for the shore. As we explained earlier, ownership of the land should not be in your own name because that could link the property, and you, to the life you are trying to escape from and maybe also the opposition. The chapter on asset anonymization offers some suggestions for property ownership, so we refer you to that section to decide what best suits you.

Location is a crucial factor in the selection of a parcel of land. The climate should not be too cold or too dry. Not only does a cold climate cause a much larger expenditure of energy to heat a home, but solar panels alone may not be sufficient, and you may have to rely on power generators. Extreme cold may also force you to rely on the services of other people, thereby creating exposure for your privacy project. In cold weather, your workload would increase while the food grow-ing season would be shortened. Arid climates are not ideal either because of the lack of water necessary to grow food plants and fruit trees, and neither are areas that regularly experience torrential rains.

The property should be in a private setting, well away from densely populated areas and definitely not in a subdivi-sion with covenants and other restrictions. Close neighbors would definitely be a liability. But your land should not be too isolated either because too much seclusion could increase your driving and reliance on outsiders in case of need or emergencies. Being close enough to urban centers also means an opportunity to do more walking and bike riding, and that is good for your health, for the planet, and for your privacy because it can reduce your car dependence, even if you have one. Proximity to an international border would be an asset in case you need an emergency escape. Too close to the border, however, can be a liability because it can increase visibility of the property and monitoring of its occupants. Sometimes land sitting on borders comes up for sale, but those properties should not be considered because they can involve the presence of border patrols and electronic surveillance. Those properties can also be subjected to eminent domain; that is, the government could expropriate them to build fences or other barriers. In choosing a land parcel, you should try to be on a hill rather than being on level terrain or in a valley. That position will give you more control over your surroundings and especially a better vantage point to check access roads or driveways leading to the property.

A property acquired for the purpose of survival and sustenance in a private and anonymous setting can be of any size, but one acre would be reasonable. Half an acre would be the absolute minimum to sustain a small family. Much over a couple of acres would be unnecessary and increase maintenance and expense. That is unless you need more land as a buffer.

Once the property is acquired, fencing should be the first order of business. A 6-foot-high chain-link fence would be adequate. More elaborate fences that are visible from a distance would generate too much attention. On the inside and against the fence, evergreen, fast-growing vegetation should be planted after fertilizing the soil appropriately and adding growth stimulants. Bamboos would be ideal for most climates. Additional plants should be added for defensive purposes as is detailed below.

Next to the vegetation screen, a footpath at least 3 feet wide should be created along the entire perimeter of the property. It should be level and preferably covered with small stone gravel to limit mud during rainy periods. On the northeast corner of the property, or wherever is most appropriate in your specific setting, a tree house or observation tower (you can refer to it as a bird-watching post, as that term may be more acceptable) could be built and painted in such a way as to blend in with the surrounding terrain and trees.

Assuming prevailing northwesterly winds and the main gate on the south end of the property, a deep pond should be created on the northwestern corner of the lot, next to the footpath. It should be no larger than one-fifth of the entire property. Using as an example a two-acre lot, the pond should be about 18,000 square feet, that is a little more than 130 x 130 feet. The metric equivalent would be approximately 40 x 40 meters. Immediately to the southeast of the pond, a level area of at least 2,000 square feet should be cleared and kept open with regular mowing of the grass. That area could be used as an emergency helipad, positioned for helicopter takeoff against prevailing winds from the helipad and over the pond. Such a helipad would come in handy in case of an emergency, such as an injury or the approaching of the opposition. It is not recommended that a helicopter be kept there, even if the owner of the property could afford it and happens to have a helicopter license. All aircraft is highly regulated and creates undesirable paper trails. It is sufficient that a list of charter operators be kept and maintained current. The open area could also be used for the waste system of the house, including buried tanks and a leach field.

South of the heliport, a small house could be built to accommodate the needs of the family occupying the property. There is no specific design that is needed for this project. If security is a concern, however, sturdy walls and small windows with gates on the lower level may be necessary. It could also have a "widow's walk," that is a deck in the center of the roof that serves as an observation point. Such decks were used in olden times in houses built along coastlines for use by wives of sea captains to search the horizon for signs of their husbands' missing ships. In an off-the-grid project, such a deck could be used to monitor surrounding areas and particularly roads leading to the property. That would be in addition to the observation tower, with the added benefit of ready access from the interior of the house. It could also be used as a platform to mount some major hardware you may need for defense and as a launch pad for a drone, assuming, of course, that it is legal in that location.

The color of the house, and particularly the observation deck, should preferably be a light green to better blend with the surrounding vegetation. The roof of the house should be covered with solar panels connected to battery banks in the lower level of the house or appropriate enclosure. The roof should also serve to catch rainwater, which would flow down from the downspouts toward a buried water tank on the west side of the house. That water tank should serve to partially fulfill the water needs of the house. The overflow, however, should be piped directly into the pond. Most of the lot should also be graded in such a way as to lead rainwater toward the pond. The water flow could also be helped by creating shallow channels, covered by gravel or other material, that would protect the channel from erosion. To the east side of the house, a vegetable garden could be established for growing basic sustenance plants. All other areas of the property not occupied should be planted with easy-to-care-for fruit trees.

The landscape assumptions in the above-described project model place the road and driveway leading to the property on the south side of the lot. The main gate should obviously be at the end of the driveway, also on the south side of the lot. A doghouse should be placed next to the gate and the footpath, with the entrance facing the gate. The only other gate should be a narrow one on the diametrically opposite side of the property, approximately a few feet from the observation tower. In that area, a toolshed can also be placed. A footpath should connect the watchtower, back gate, and toolshed to the back entrance of the house, going over the heliport area.

The pond would serve several functions. One would be irrigation of the vegetable garden and fruit trees during periods of dry weather. That is normally accomplished by the use of a pump and multi-prong hoses that reach the base of each tree as well as sprinklers and other devices for the vegetable garden. Fish farming is another purpose of this type of pond. In particular cases, one can also use water from the pond for human needs in and around the house with appropriate filtration.

Constructing a pond is not difficult and does not need to be expensive. There are in fact many cases in which people have built one almost for free, by letting nature do its thing. Digging a pond, however, needs to be part of the overall grading of the lot because it is necessary to employ the excavated dirt in such a way as to elevate the area where the house and other improvements are going to be placed and create a slope toward the pond. After the initial dig, a berm needs to be placed around the pond, making allowance for entry points for water flowing down to the pond from higher ground. A discharge for excess water needs to be placed on the opposite side of the pond, going over the footpath and away from the house. To avoid erosion and disturbance of the footpath, a paved channel needs to be built with a mini bridge over it for foot and dog traffic.

Before filling the pond, a soil test needs to be performed to determine if water leakage problems are to be expected. If so, clay material needs to be spread over the bottom of the pond and maybe even the sides of it. If the soil is extremely porous, the bottom may need to be lined with plastic sheeting. With some luck, however, those measures will not be needed. The next step will be to plant algae, which will be underwater once the pond is filled. If the lot has been graded properly and rain is abundant, the pond will naturally fill within a short time. In a low-rain season, it may be necessary to spend a considerable amount of money to have water delivered to the site. That is why the timing of pond construction is a key component of planning.

As soon as the pond is full, the first batch of small fish can be introduced. One or more bug zapper lamps should then be mounted on top of poles protruding above the pond. During the hot weather season, or always in a tropical locale, the insects killed by the lamps will fall into the pond. The dead insects, along with algae and other nutrients, will feed the small fish. As soon as a viable colony of small fish is established, a batch of larger fish can gradually be introduced. The larger fish will feed on the small fish and other food that can be artificially provided for them from various sources, including leaves and small branches that come from pruning trees. The larger fish can occasionally form part of your sustenance.

In a large lot located in the tropics, a bug zap light or two will not be sufficient to eliminate insects. And if you are doing organic farming, insects are a huge problem, not only as a nuisance to humans but also as a threat to vegetables and fruit trees. A potential fix for that is the erection of a pole with a bat house on top in an appropriate location. Bats are nature's best pesticide and do not harm humans. But it is crucial to select the right species of bats you intend to introduce. You need bats that only eat insects and not the species that like fruit or a combination of fruit and insects. Go for the strictly carnivores.

A useful addition to your operation could be chicken farming to supplement the protein that the occasional fish can provide. Be careful, however, about zoning regulations. Many areas near urban centers ban chickens. If you violate zoning regulations, you are going to attract the attention of neighbors and possibly the law.

If you are balancing the forces of nature correctly, when the off-the-grid project is fully functioning, you will have created your own ecosystem that can provide basic survival for you and your family.

If you are someone facing a serious opposition and are concerned for your safety, security becomes a necessity. Security, however, is not an absolute concept, just as there is no way you can ensure safety one hundred percent. But there is a lot you can do to protect yourself and your loved ones without breaking the bank or relying on professional companies.

The chain-link fence mentioned above by itself will do little to prevent a determined intruder, but it nevertheless constitutes a physical and legal barrier. In order to enter your property, an intruder will need to use tools and thereby trespass by breaking and entering, which is a crime for which she can be arrested. The fence is also a visual demarcation line that warns people to stay away and behind which the real security devices are installed and planted. Electrifying the fence may be a good idea as long as it does not affect friendly humans or the dogs. But the "welcome committee" would not be complete without the addition of "defensive" and even "offensive" plants. Defensive plants feature thorns or spiky leaves that can scratch or puncture the skin. They discourage trespassers and even some animals from walking through them. Offensive plants are actually dangerous to humans and animals in that they are poisonous or can trigger severe allergic reactions. If you add those to the "reception committee," make sure that your family and pets do not approach them.

The Agave is a slow growing succulent that can create a barrier that is difficult to get through. The leaves are spiny or serrated, and the end forms a very sharp point that can pierce the flesh. Sometimes, the sharp point breaks off and embeds itself deep in the skin. Serious injury would result from contact with an eye. Blackberries are another good choice because once the plant is in the ground, it will grow quickly. Combine this growth speed with the multiple thorns covering the entire plant, and you have the perfect defensive barrier. Few people would dare to walk through a blackberry patch. Another good choice is the Cholla Cactus. Covered in extremely sharp spines that detach and stick into clothing and flesh, it could prove a challenge for any would-be intruder. The Devil's Walking Stick has thick, twisted branches with long, sharp spikes. It grows to about 20 feet tall but can be pruned regularly into a hedge ready to stab anyone trying to get through. The Crown of Thorns, or Jesus plant, grows to about 6 feet. The flowers are red, white, or pink and often bloom all year round; but underneath that, the thorns are vicious and plentiful.

Hardy Orange is a perfect perimeter plant, and can also be used as a buffer in that it is a fast-growing tree that can reach

90 feet in height. Mesquite plants have long spikes, a rugged, twisted trunk, and small blue or green leaves. The Honey Locust is an aggressive plant that develops into a bush filled with thorns unless you prune it to limit it to a single trunk. If you do train it like this, there is no way anyone will climb it to get a vantage point on your property. The Prickly Pear plant is one of the best defensive choices. It has two lines of defense: first is the obvious rows of thorns that will stick into your skin even through clothing; second is the fine hair-like fibers that dig into you and are near impossible to remove. They hurt just as much as the big spikes.

Among offensive plants is the Manchineel, a tree whose leaves and fruits resemble those of an apple, and it is sometimes known innocuously as "beach apple." However, its Spanish name, "*manzanilla de la* muerte" ("little apple of death"), better reflects its dangerous properties. The plant contains a number of toxins, and eating its fruits could possibly kill you and will certainly blister your mouth and esophagus. The milky sap of the leaves and bark contains an irritating chemical called phorbol, which generates a strong allergic skin reaction. Even raindrops falling through the tree can absorb phorbol and burn a person standing underneath. Native people would use the sap for poison arrows. Poison Ivy and its close relatives, Poison Sumac and Poison Oak, contain a chemical known as urushiol. When touched, nearly all parts of these plants can trigger a severe, itchy, and painful inflammation of the skin. Even more frighteningly, urushiol can persist on clothing, shoes, tools, soil, or animals that have made contact with the plants, thus potentially poisoning additional victims.

Stinging Nettle features leaves and stems with stinging hairs tipped with an acid substance and other irritants. If touched, these hairs inject the stinging acid into the skin, triggering a burning, tingling sensation and an itchy rash. Tread-Softly is a plant covered with stinging hairs that can also cause skin irritation if touched. That is because the hairs that penetrate the skin release nasty irritants. Giant Hogweed generates a sap that can cause phytophotodermatitis, in which the skin severely blisters if exposed to the sun, and can result in blindness if the sap enters the eyes.

Gympie-Gympie would be an extreme option for your fence. It is a potentially lethal species of Australian stinging tree. Among stinging plants, none is quite as aggressive as the Gympie-Gympie. This is one of the most dangerous plants in the world. The stinging leaves trigger an intense allergic reaction in its victims, sometimes even causing anaphylactic shock. The sting can cause excruciating, debilitating pain for months; people have variously described it as feeling like they are being electrocuted, burned by acid, or crushed by giant hands. Another option in this category is the African Poison Ivy, also known as the Pain Bush. It is native to southern Africa and lives up to its name. The plant is a small tree or shrub and exudes a creamy sap that is laden with chemicals known as heptadecyl catechols.

The footpath along the fence can provide an easy way to control the perimeter on foot, on a bike, or walking a guard dog. As far as guard dogs are concerned, you will need to make important choices. You need at least one but preferably two. If you get a second dog, it should not be housed together with the one living in the doghouse near the main gate but in a separate doghouse near the back gate.

Dogs should be trained to regularly walk the perimeter of the property on the footpath as if on patrol. It should also be kept in mind that not all dogs are created equal. When it comes to protecting your property and your family, there are several types of dogs. Some are barkers, meaning they will let you know when something or someone moves around your home that is not supposed to be there. Then there are guard dogs proper. These breeds will not only let you know if someone approaches the house, but they will also do something about it. Those are the ones you want.

Among the best guard dogs is the Akita, an intense and intelligent breed–very loyal to its owner but not so friendly to strangers. The German Shepherd is also very intense and loyal and will not hesitate to attack someone threatening you or your property. The Doberman Pinscher is a phenomenal animal. It has short hair, which makes it suitable for warm climates. It is very intelligent and loyal. And it is so powerful, agile, and fierce-looking that it usually does not even need to attack. An intruder will normally give up and choose an easier property to rob. Like the Doberman, the Rottweiler can probably get away with guarding your property on its looks alone. It is usually a little larger than the Doberman but perhaps not as agile. The Dogo Argentino, or Argentine Mastiff, is large and muscular. Its short hair makes it suitable for warm climates. Though originally bred for hunting, the dog is powerful and fearless so can easily be used as a guard dog.

An effective surveillance system will include video cameras located at strategic points on your property. Some of them can be equipped with long-range night vision that can let you monitor a dark environment as far as tens of feet away. Motion security systems are economical and easy to install next to a house. Ground-based radar systems can have a range up to 15,000 feet or more. Some companies sell complete perimeter surveillance systems. They usually work by using two cameras, one high definition and one a thermal-imaging camera. This is bundled with special software to provide a seamless perimeter security. If your budget is limited and you are facing an impending threat, a very low-tech solution is the old-fashioned nylon string connected to objects such as empty cans that can make noise when dropped or banged against each other. The line, which can be a thin fishing line, is almost invisible unless you are looking for it, especially at night. You could run it around poles placed a few feet from the house and at a height of at least 4 feet.

You may want to have a few security items handy in the house. One is a pair of night goggles, also known as NOD that stands for night/optical observation device. That device allows images to be produced in levels of light approaching total darkness. The image may be a conversion to visible light of both visible light and near-infrared. The image produced is typically monochrome, that is in shades of green. If you need to do a personal reconnaissance of the property at night, a NOD can be very helpful. Another item that can be of great help if you believe you hear something in the distance, especially in the dark, but are afraid to venture out, is a long-range hearing device. The device is technically low tech. It is made of a parabolic dish of about 1 foot or 16 inches in diameter. At the center of it is a very sensitive microphone that is connected to headphones. All you need to do is point the dish in the direction of the sound or voice you want to investigate. The sound magnifying power of this simple device is amazing.

If you enjoy exotic pets and the challenges that come with them, you can buy a baby alligator or crocodile, even online for a very reasonable price. They sell them with food pellets that can last a long time. The alligator can thrive in a tropical or subtropical environment and would love your pond. As babies, they measure only a foot or two, but they can grow up to 3 feet per year if you take care of them. In truth, these animals do not exactly bond with humans, but they get used to their environment and their feeder. In normal circumstances, they do not pose a threat to humans. But they are not necessarily going to be friendly with a stranger poking around the property and their territory. And the visuals these beasts can provide can be as powerful as their physical strength. Nothing says "get out of here" better than a 14-foot reptile staring at you in silence.

We do not recommend this but, if you have money to burn and do not mind giving up the ecological balance offered by the pond and sustenance from fish farming, there is another thing you can do to increase security. When you dig the pond and grade the lot, you could also dig a deep moat around the property, connected with the pond. It would need to be at least 5 feet wide and 6 feet deep and run along the footpath, inside the fence. An intruder who cuts the fence will need to wade through the moat to get inside the property. The only interruption of the circular moat would be the main entrance gate and that is where the doghouse would be located and, hence, the dog when he is not on patrol. That would mean additional security for the width of the gate, so that an intruder will have no choice but to wade. And a memorable bath it could be if you stock the pond and moat with amphibious snakes and fresh water predators such as piranhas. And speaking of predators, if you regularly feed your alligator where the moat ends by the main gate, the animal would hang out there most of the time and make a pretty good visual sentry. You would have to hope, however, that it gets along with the dog. In any event, you should see the dog as a working animal and not just a companion to sit on your lap. That would make for a more efficient defense animal, and it would also make it easier to accept its loss.

Between tending the fruit trees, the vegetable garden, the pond, and all other needs of the land, there may not be a lot of time left for hobbies. But flying a drone can be a rewarding experience that could give you a chance to do some serious bird and nature watching. And in case of need, it can help you monitor traffic approaching the property beyond the range possible with other security equipment. Drones can also be rigged to carry a payload. We advise you to check with your lawyer before flying any equipment, but note that Amazon is already testing deliveries by drone to their customers. Maybe you too could deliver a package to the approaching opposition and thus end the threat it poses to you once and for all.

In the following chapters, you will learn that living off the grid can be achieved in a permanent house as well as in a mobile home, trailer, motorhome, tent; or even on a boat. The choice is dictated by the area where you travel from or going to, your budget, climate, and personal skills and preferences. Every alternative tends to have pros and cons, but a careful analysis in the end will dictate the appropriate solution.

The property layout in the example above would be ideal for a permanent house but also for an RV, or for both. More on RVs in the following chapter, but some considerations apply here. An RV meant to be used as a permanent residence should probably be large enough to ensure long-term comfort. But it should also be self-propelled and parked in a location that is free of obstructions and near the property gate. It should always be parked with the nose towards the gate so as to facilitate an emergency departure.

An auxiliary vehicle–that is in addition to a house–could be smaller, and we would recommend a camper van or a very small motorhome. In all cases, the RV should always be kept in good condition. The tires should be inflated, the batteries charged, and the fuel and water tanks full. The vehicle should be fully equipped, and essentials should be on board at all times. The idea is that, in case you need to make a quick exit, you don't need to spend time looking for tools or sorting your wardrobe.

EIGHT

THE VANISHING ACT

---

1. Planning and Ground Work

The general thrust of this book is on planning in advance for a possible future exit from an ordinary or troubled life. The reasons for a vanishing act can be many, but the actual disappearance may never take place and instead remain a fantasy. Either way, just the planning stage takes a lot of time and preparation. And it can be a lot of fun. Of course, life is not perfect, and there can be circumstances in which one needs to take immediate action. In this chapter, we are proposing a proper sequence of the actions you need to take for a seamless and perfect exit. You can, of course, adjust the plan to fit your particular circumstances.

If you consider all of the ties and entanglements that form part of everyday life, you will see that just about all of them have been created by you. That is of course normal in most circumstances. But if you need or want to become anonymous and disappear, then you will need to reevaluate all the ties that form the web of your existence. The first thing to look at is relationships. Perhaps it is one or more of those relationships or their failure that is driving you away. If not, then you need to consider your relationship to the people that matter the most to you. Can you live without them? Can you bear to cease all communications when you are gone? This is an existential question because a vanishing act is generally not for a group, family, or even a couple. In this business, you generally travel solo and do not look back. The minute you make a phone call to someone in your network from the Land of the Disappeared, the opposition is likely to track you down. Maybe they have been patiently waiting for you to break down and make that crucial mistake. If you are not ready to cut all ties, do not even try a vanishing act because you will surely fail.

After evaluating your personal relationships, you need to look at your business and extended social network, with a view to cut those links as well. It would be a mistake, however, to suddenly drop out. The best strategy is to gradually withdraw. Cut down on phone calls, texts, and emails. You then need to start taking down your online social networks like Facebook, X, Instagram, WhatsApp, TikTok, Meetups, and wherever else you have been active. That, too, should not be an abrupt termination. You can start by not responding to messages or delay your replies and ignore posts. You decrease your activity until you take down everything. If you have a social life that revolves around certain groups, friends, or activities, start going out less and less. The main goal of your gradual withdrawal is to deconstruct your persona among your friends, business associates, or even family. Ideally, you should take longer and longer trips out of town until the time you never return. Think of this process not as disappearing but fading away. For once, you should hope not to be missed.

Slowly but surely, you should start withdrawing cash from your bank accounts in varying amounts. Do not wait until you are on the road because that would give the opposition a map of your itinerary. And we hope that you have cash to take out because, if you do not, your life in the Land of the Disappeared may end sooner than you think and probably badly–assuming you even get to your destination.

If you live with other people, like roommates, all of your personal items must eventually be removed, but you must be careful how you do this. Examples of items to be removed include documents, cards, photographs, computers, old phones, flash drives, mail and bills, files, notebooks, address books, car and insurance documents, medicines, old glasses, and even books. The removal of those items is necessary because almost everything you leave behind can tell something about you, even a lot–not to mention your fingerprints!

Things you own can tell who you are, where you have been, and where you are likely to go next. An immense wealth of information already exists on you through online records of your shopping, travel, dating, email correspondence, website visits, online applications, medical history, and forum participation. Those records are almost impossible to erase. But you can at least make it harder for the opposition to connect all of the dots. Depending on your particular situation, after you are gone, there is a strong possibility that the opposition will visit your house. Every item you have left behind can offer leads as to your intentions and your plan.

The next step you need to take, and you should give that priority, is to advise the postman that you are moving and can no longer collect your mail. Every account, billing, and anything that requires you to receive mail must be moved online, or preferably closed. In this day and age, it is not unusual for people to not receive snail mail, so that should be your general approach as well. You should contact directly any company that sends you mail to make sure they stop sending it. As you progress with your groundwork, you should get to the point where you no longer need to receive mail. If there is anything you absolutely need to receive after you are gone, and we strongly discourage it, you can get a post office box, in the manner recommended in the chapter on privacy. For all junk mail, and that is all you should be receiving post-vanishing, you can file a change of address with the post office listing your new address in a faraway, imaginary location. That will have the dual benefit of stopping the mail from coming to your old address and creating a red herring for the opposition. You can be certain that they will check mail delivery, and that is why setting up a real post office box at this stage is such a bad idea.

If you are employed, it would be good form and also to your benefit for you to not just drop out. It is better to start complaining about the job and expressing general dissatisfaction. You should approach the boss and discuss a possible termination and severance pay. The idea behind this approach is not only to leave your affairs in order but also to create false leads as to why you may have left.

If you have not had a physical exam in a while, this is a good time to do it. Get a dental checkup and if there are any issues, resolve them. If you wear glasses, get an extra pair. If you take any medicines, refill them now. If you are not in great shape, use this preparation time to do some exercise. Practice jogging and running; do basic motion exercises without hurting yourself. When the time comes to make your move, you should be as fit as you can manage to get. Good health and a certain level of fitness can greatly help in the uncertain road you are about to take.

As we said earlier, less is more, and that is particularly true at this stage of your planning. This is a great time to shed unnecessary clothing, furniture items, mementos no longer important, and everything you see around you that you can live without. Not only do you not want to leave any clues to the opposition, but you also want moving day to be a non-event. You should never hire a moving company to move your possessions to your destination because they keep records and may also remember you. Enlisting the help of friends would also be a huge mistake. Neighbors can notice your move as will your housemates, if you have any. The best strategy is to anonymously rent storage space in a different part of town or in the next town over. That storage is for the gradual move of the items you absolutely need to take to the Land of the Disappeared. Those should be as few as possible. Better to sell, throw out, or donate.

If you have a car, it can help you during preparations for your disappearance, and maybe during the first stage of your journey. After that it will become a huge liability. If you will not use the car to get away and don't really use it regularly, you should consider selling it. You will need the cash wherever you are going. You also don't want to leave any assets to the opposition. If they are related to you and have a right to use the car, that may add it to their resources. Fingerprints and other personal information can be obtained by searching a vehicle. If you are not going to use the car to get away and you can't sell it, you should consider disabling it permanently or junking it. People used to put sugar in the tank to destroy the engine, but that is a rather slow process. They now have liquids you can buy that will kill the engine outright. Alternatively, you can drive the car to a neighborhood where theft is rampant and leave it unlocked with the keys in the ignition. Who knows, you might even get some insurance money to help you in your travels.

If you own real estate, you have some hard choices ahead of you. As we explained in the section in this book on assets, it is generally a mistake to own assets in your name. But if you already have them in your name, the best course of action would be to sell them. If you own a house free and clear, that is without any mortgage or loan, you can transfer it to a corporation or LLC for a later sale. That would be better than placing it in a trust because you could eventually make corporate changes that remove yourself from the corporation. In that way, your signature and your presence would not be required at the time of sale. In many cases, you can sell real estate in the name of a corporation by selling the shares of the corporation. That transaction leaves no record in the land and property registers. The only changes, theoretically at least, are the tax consequences of any capital gains. But that may be too much information for you at this point–seriously!

Throughout your preparations, you should not lose sight of one crucial matter. Not only should you avoid telling people that you are planning to disappear, but you should also avoid discussions with friends and family about places where you would like to go, if those places include your actual intended destination. Any specific destination that you have mentioned to family and friends would effectively rule it out for your final plan. Not only should you not discuss a destination or modality of travel, but you should also not even research it on your computer. For the reasons we have discussed earlier, your Internet searches are not a secret for those with access. Therefore, if you have been searching online for real estate, say, in Margaritaville or, God forbid, already had negotiations about the purchase of a property there, you should rule that place out completely. Any research you need to make relating to your plans must be done either at an anonymous Internet location such as a public library or by using an anonymous device in a place with open Wi-Fi. If the device has ever been used in any manner that can connect it to you, such as your home Internet provider, for example, you should assume that the device is no longer safe and neither is your online research.

After deconstructing your old self, if you haven't already done so, you need to start planning for the future and reinvent yourself. If you are going to assume a new identity and make all of the changes that that process entails, this is the time to get it done; and we refer you to the section on identities, but make sure you check with your lawyer first.

Unless you are independently wealthy, you should start thinking about a job or business in the Land of the Disappeared. Unless you are able and willing to do manual work along with undocumented aliens, any employer is going to ask you for documents and references. It is, therefore, much preferable to become self-employed. If you have experience in carpentry, plumbing, graphic design, photography, or any other marketable trade, you should be able to set up a business, as long as you are going to an urban area with normal economic activity. If you do not have any practical skills, you may want to take some classes to acquire the skills that you will need in your new life.

Whatever business you get into, you should use a corporation such as an LLC. Never use your own name, even if you have a brand new one. This is the time to form a few corporations and LLCs to use as your new incarnations in the Land of the Disappeared. If you need a bank account and the use of a name and signature is required, you can try using an LLC with a name that resembles yours. Let's say you are calling yourself Alfred Bruce Loomis. You could set up something called Alfred B. Loomis, LLC. In time, that could become AB Loomis, LLC; and then A. Bloomis, LLC. For all intents and purposes, that could eventually become your signature. To get ahead of the game and make sure you hit the ground running when you get to the Land of the Disappeared, you can start printing business cards and brochures. But make sure you do not use your local printer. You can also start making preliminary arrangements for a place to live and a business address or post office box number. For that you may need advance visits to your final destination, but be careful not to leave any trails.

The clothes that you often wear should be discarded, especially if they are unique. If you wear long hair, you may want to cut it, but do so in stages. You may also want to buy hair coloring agents to be used at the time of your departure. But it should not be a drastic color change, just in case you run into someone you know as you leave. You can complete the job when you reach the Land of the Disappeared. It is important to dispose properly of any items you use for hair coloring well away from your house.

If you have read this far, we should not have to remind you to pay for all critical purchases in cash. And, speaking of purchases, you should buy a prepaid phone for emergencies, and make sure you do that in a location that is far away from your house and not connected to you. The same goes for prepaid debit cards. You will need those, as you must cut up all of your current debit and credit cards as soon as you make your last withdrawal. It is better not to even have the temptation to use an old credit card.

As we mentioned above, using your car for your entire journey to the Land of the Disappeared would be very dangerous. But you might decide to use it for part of the trip and, if you do, you should try to take the following precautions. Find a garage or storage area well away from your part of town. You can then buy masking tape, brushes, roller brushes, primer, and polyurethane paint of a color different from your car's color. In a few hours, you can mask the car windows, lights, and trim. You can then apply a coat of the primer and, as soon as it dries, one coat or two of the polyurethane paint. For large areas, you use the roller, and for smaller areas, the brush. It's that simple. It is amazing how polyurethane paint levels itself as if it had been sprayed on. In no time, you will have a new car. Not a perfect job, but it can pass from a distance. You then remove the plates and replace them with other plates you can get from a junkyard. But be very careful when you drive your "new" car and only do it if absolutely necessary. Police routinely check car plates while they are behind you, and if things do not check out, you are in for a bad day. You also do not want to drive the car back home after the paint job. Park it a few blocks away so that it will be out of sight of neighbors but ready for you when you hit the road. Before you leave the car for the last time until travel day, take a substantial amount of time to wipe off all surfaces with rubbing alcohol. Start from the trunk, and work your way forward. Every single item which is *touchable* must be cleaned of prints. Doing this in advance will make things easier on travel day.

An important part of your preparations should involve packing, and you should take that very seriously. While your general plan may call for an easy journey to your dream destination, things may go differently. There are items you are not contemplating as being required by your plan that may end up saving your life. One item you should always have around and keep in a safe but easily accessible place is a "panic bag."

People who live dangerously or on boats always keep such a bag. It should contain a passport and other documents; cash (including in the currencies of countries you plan to visit); essential medicines; an emergency kit; a thermal blanket; address books either digital or physical; a pad and pen; a burner phone; spare glasses; a flashlight; a Swiss Army knife; a box of matches; water; and sealed, nutritious snacks. And if you own a gun, it should be kept in the bag as well. But if you plan to fly, which we do not recommend, checking in weapons even if legal can attract attention. High caliber rifles with scopes and silencers are a definite no-no. No matter how good your intentions, the scrutiny these weapons will bring can work against you.

It is actually a good idea for anyone to keep a panic bag. It can be useful in case of fires, natural disasters, terrorism, unexpected government action, and other emergencies. If you are planning a vanishing act due to some pressing issues you are facing, it is always possible that things will come to a head sooner than you think. Your panic bag should, therefore, also contain other items, including a basic change of clothes (including warmer clothes) than you normally expect to wear, in case of your being forced to overnight outdoors. Some camouflage clothing could also help, but its use should be limited to circumstances where it is actually needed. Additional recommended devices for an emergency departure are a GPS device (not your actual phone, for the reasons we have explained earlier) and a short-wave receiver. Since the emergency phone you will be carrying will be turned off, you will need to carry a watch and possibly a compass. It should be something easily readable and fluorescent. Batteries should be kept separate from all transmitting devices and only inserted in them when needed.

As your departure approaches, you should decide exactly what you will be wearing and set it aside. Try to get a weather forecast to assess the possibility of a cold snap or serious rain. Common sense applies to your choice of clothing. That should include shoes that are very comfortable and can handle wet or slippery surfaces. A hat or cap is a real necessity because if you can pull down the visor, you can hide your face from CCTV cameras and other monitoring equipment that rely on your face to identify you. For defensive purposes, you should plan to carry a knife, in addition to the Swiss Army knife. It should not be in a bag but should be carried on your person, so that will go on top of the pile of clothes to be worn.

Another essential task to prepare for your new life is to build a "legend," that is a history of your presumptive past. The legend should be compatible with your age, appearance, language, ethnic background, and other biographical details. If, for example, you are a mainstream Canadian from Toronto, you could probably pass for an American from, say, Michigan and vice versa. Your legend should include educational background, memories, and "family" pictures. You will need all of those details in your future conversations in the Land of the Disappeared. You should definitely visit the place you will claim as your hometown and become very familiar with it. Memorize landmarks and take a lot of pictures to review later. Visit restaurants, schools, shops, and establishments that were in business when you were supposed to be there. Exercise mentally to start thinking of that place as your real hometown. Get in the zone.

2. Forensics 101

A discussion on basic forensics applies both to the preparation stage and travel day in your vanishing act. It can also apply to many other situations where you are trying to avoid leaving signs of your presence or transit.

Forensic science is the application of science to criminal and civil laws. What police officers and investigators do is to collect, preserve, and analyze scientific evidence. Some of this is done at the scene of a crime or other event, but the rest of the analysis is usually done in a laboratory.

The main tool of a forensic test, at least in the popular imagination, is the use of fingerprints, which can be easily traced on most surfaces that have been touched by a human. Forensic DNA analysis has been in use for over 30 years. A test can involve saliva, blood, or semen, but also skin and other biological matter. DNA databases have been created over the years. There is a national FBI database for the U.S., and other international databases such as ENFSI, which stands for the European Network of Forensic Science Institutes. Those searchable databases are used to match crime scene DNA profiles to those already in the database. In recent years, documenting forensics scenes has become more efficient. Investigators have started using laser scanners, drones, and photogrammetry to obtain 3D point images of accidents or crime scenes. Reconstruction of an accident scene on a highway using drones involves a data acquisition time of only 10-20 minutes and can be performed without shutting down traffic. The results are not just accurate, but also easy to digitally preserve. Traces of someone's presence or activity can also be gained from other identifiers such as tooth marks, among other things.

Without going into all of the details of this complex discipline, you should be aware that forensic science, and much more than we can summarize here, can be brought to bear in an investigation of your disappearance, and aid in predicting your itinerary if you are on the move. So, pay particular attention to traces and clues you inadvertently leave behind. Wherever you go, you can leave traces. Everything you touch, every piece of clothing, every toilet seat you use, every hair you drop will contain your DNA. If you lick an envelope, you will leave DNA, and if you touch the envelope you just licked, you will leave fingerprints as well. It cannot be stressed enough how important it is to carefully plan a disappearance that leaves as few clues and traces as possible.

3. Run Baby Run

If you have carefully prepared your plan, at this point, you should be almost ready to go. You should pick a time to leave when no one is home, and your neighbors are not likely to be out and about. Hopefully, you have chosen a day, or night, without weather emergencies. An ice storm, snowstorm, or torrential rain will make things a lot more difficult, and we don't just mean inconvenient. Your movement would be slowed down. If in a car, you would risk an accident, and on foot you could get drenched or very cold. You could slip on ice. If any of those weather events is taking place, the best course of action is to abort your departure.

Your house should have been thoroughly cleaned with most of your fingerprints and other DNA traceable clues removed. All of the excess baggage should be gone, either discarded far away or in storage. All you should be carrying on your way out is the panic bag. You should be wearing neutral or new clothes that you have prepared in advance. Hopefully, you are feeling well with all major issues resolved or under control. About 1 hour before you leave, you should have a nutritious meal but not a heavy one. Avoid drinking coffee, alcohol, and too much water. Place your last trash in a small bag, and place it in the panic bag so that you can dispose of it later.

It comes naturally in our daily lives to touch many things, but you can't afford to leave prints just now. You need to use rubbing alcohol on all surfaces and objects you may have touched. Rubbing alcohol wipes out the natural oils that comprise most fingerprints. As soon as everything has been wiped clean, you should put on gloves. You should also avoid wearing shoes until you are on the pavement outside the house. Heavy socks are all you should be wearing so as not to leave shoe prints anywhere. While this may sound paranoid, it actually is not. Anyone looking for you in a professional way will be trying to match your shoes and shoe prints with prints found in locations where they suspect you may be or have been. Since there is no database of footprints, all the opposition will have to go by is what you leave behind. And we are assuming and hoping here that you will not be leaving shoes behind.

There are many ways to get away from your home and head for the Land of the Disappeared. The choice will be determined by your particular situation, the geography of the area, the availability of public transportation, the vehicle or vehicles at your disposal, and many other factors.

Let us start with the form of travel that we do not recommend. Taxis are a bad choice. Drivers and dispatchers make records of people they pick up and drop off. Drivers may also remember you. For Uber, Lyft, and similar car services you need an app on your phone to schedule a ride and that creates a digital record of the trip as well as charges on a credit card. Of course, you could use a prepaid card based on a nickname, but you are still adding a searchable trail. If you can get far enough away from your home and hail a cab from there, that might be a better option but not a perfect one. That is unless you live in a metropolis.

Having a friend drive you would also be a bad move. Your friend will know all about your plan and that leaves you exposed. You never can tell what people will do under intense pressure. Hitchhiking would be problematic and time consuming, even assuming you are in an area where you can get a ride. Under no circumstance should you use a moving van or truck. That is for later. A moving truck will alert neighbors, and of course people living in your house. The driver and helpers might remember you. If you rent a truck and drive it yourself, you will have to return it, which creates yet another complication. Of course your neighbors will see a rental truck just as they will see a moving company truck. Avoiding a last-day move of your personal effects is the reason why, in your preparation stage, you need to gradually move or dispose of everything you have.

Depending on how far you plan to go, you might use a bicycle, or even walk. You could walk or bike to a bus or train station, if practical. A motorcycle may be an option but not a very good one. First of all, you would need to be able to ride the motorcycle even in challenging conditions, which can include weather events and hot pursuits. Motorcycles are also not as common as other vehicles on the road and that makes them more likely to be noticed. In addition, law enforcement tends to pay more attention to motorcycles as they are traditionally associated with gangs and criminal activities. All that makes it more likely to get stopped.

Realistically, at least for the beginning of the trip, your best bet might be to use your car, after making the modifications we discussed earlier. The car should be in perfect working order as you can't afford stopping for mechanical help at this stage of your life. Nor can you afford to get pulled over by a patrol. You therefore have to make sure that your brake lights and turn signals work. Make sure you have enough fuel in the tank, air in the tires, and that the fluids levels are where they should be. Your car should not be loaded with your personal possessions. You want to look like someone on a regular errand or a commuter. The car should not be parked by your house but several blocks away. Since you have painted it, it might attract the curiosity of neighbors who are used to seeing the same vehicle in a different color.

As you drive off, you want to make sure you are obeying all road signs and rules. Do not speed, and do not go excessively slow. Going excessively slow could be seen by a patrol as a sign of intoxication or other problem. Relax and look straight in front of you. Do not get distracted by a phone that you should not even have. Remember that highways are full of cameras that can monitor vehicles and follow their location. If you managed to get "new" plates from, say, a local junkyard, they may give you some comfort but also a false sense of security. A patrol behind you should be cause for alarm as they can run your plates, and that would surely lead to your being pulled over. But if you act normal and do not panic, they will probably not do that. And to minimize the chances of being pulled over, it is also better to avoid areas frequented by drug dealers or prostitutes.

Your car journey should not be any longer than necessary. If the journey is a long one, you might be tempted to stop at a motel for the night. That would be a mistake as you would be giving an additional clue of your journey. If you really need to take a break, try at least to avoid motels patronized by criminals, transients, and drifters. People hanging out in the parking lot may be a sign of trouble, as would be blood stains on the walls of the room. Be careful with the registration process if you can't avoid it. Pay cash, and try not to produce your ID, especially if you are still using your birth name. The car trip should bring you in proximity of a train station or bus station or to a place, far enough from home, where you can take a taxi. But you should not go by taxi to your final destination, as the driver might remember you and the drop-off point. Another getaway strategy if you choose to use taxis is to take several so as not to leave a point-A-to-point-B transit record.

By the time you are done with the car, you need to have a plan to dispose of it in a way that it will not be found too soon. But the choices are not many. Driving it into a river or lake would probably be more trouble than it's worth. Tire marks would give the car away, and a car sunk in shallow water can usually be spotted by helicopters. Setting it on fire might attract attention and, if you get caught, also expose you to a charge of arson or reckless endangerment. You could just park the car and leave it unlocked, hoping that it gets stolen. Finally, you could deflate one tire and abandon it. For a little while, people and the police might assume that someone got a flat tire and has gone somewhere to get tools or help. If you had the perfect disposal solution at your final destination, you might try to go all of the way in your car. But, without knowing more, that would seem a very dangerous course of action. Depending on where you are going, people might observe the car, thereby placing you in jeopardy just as you arrive in the Land of the Disappeared. Whatever you do with your car, before you part with it, plan to spend some time to wipe off, one last time, surfaces you may have touched before you started using gloves. Do not forget handles, the new license plates, the emergency brake and turn signals, the steering wheel, radio controls, onboard touch pad, and any knobs and switches you may have touched. Under pressure, you may not be doing a great job of it, but most of it should have already been done during the preparation stage of your vanishing act.

The escape model we have followed would see you to your destination through a combination of walking, driving, and public transportation or taxi. It assumes that it all goes without a hitch, especially with the driving part. But things do not always go well. So let's look at some potential problem scenarios along the way.

As you are driving, you can be randomly stopped by a patrol. Or the patrol could be part of the opposition. Or a non-governmental opposition could be chasing you and somehow follow you as you are driving. If you are ordered to stop your vehicle, you will be faced with at least one existential choice. Do you take off with the car or bail out? Taking off with the car and triggering a car chase, except in rare circumstances, we think would be a folly. You might want to drive a short while to reach a more favorable terrain to escape. Or cross a bridge or other structure that somehow will give you advantage. But a car chase in itself can only end badly. If you are being followed by government authorities, you can be sure that they have backup or can call for it. They can set up roadblocks and radio your position to countless other law enforcement. Speeding in your car under those circumstances will end in an accident or in a more serious confrontation with the police, which can lead, among other things, to your arrest and extensive questioning.

Following this escape scenario, imagine that you are now pulling over on the side of the road with a patrol car behind you. Let us assume that a helicopter is on the scene or is expected to come soon. The job of the helicopter crew is to spot vehicles and their drivers. Once the vehicle stops, they will wait for the driver to come out; and if she runs, they will follow her. The handling of remaining passengers in a vehicle is normally left to police ground crews. One way to trick your pursuers and gain a few precious moments is to pretend you are a passenger when you bail out of the car. You can climb over to the rear seat, grab your panic bag, and exit from the rear door, right after you kick open the driver's door. That ruse may cause a distraction, but not a lengthy one. So from the moment you bail out of the vehicle, you are literally on the run. Run, baby, run.

As you run for your freedom or even your life, you can expect police crews to follow you. Your main task, therefore, is to outpace them and gain ground, at least until you get to some area of vegetation or other visual barriers where you can temporarily hide. The pace at which you will be able to run is going to depend on your level of fitness. But, while moving fast, you should not go into a dead run you cannot sustain. You will need reserve energy to complete your escape.

The problem with running from the police or other well-equipped opposition is that they do not just rely on the driver of a patrol car. You can bet that other agents are on the way. They will carry radios and other equipment as well as dogs. Even if you have been able to temporarily elude them, you still have a major challenge as they try to close in on you. Any sign of your presence that you leave behind can cost you dearly, so you have the additional worries of your body heat, your smell, and footprints.

As much as you need to move forward, breaking your trail a few times would make life a little harder for the dogs, who are picking up your scent, and for ground forces tracking your footprints. Breaking the trail can be done by backtracking, moving in circles, or crossing a body of water, even if only to cross it back to return to a different location on the trail. Many of the choices you make would be dictated by the terrain and the formation and proximity of the opposition. It is hard to tell whether a dense forest is better than an environment of mixed foliage and clearings or a city environment. What is clear is that a flat and treeless landscape can spell real trouble because there is nowhere to hide. But you know that before you stop the car. So that may be the rare situation where you decide to drive on until you can see possibilities to hide.

Ideally, you are moving in the direction of your destination or at least toward some transportation hub where you can hop on a train or bus. But if the chase looks dire for you, with the opposition coming at you from different directions, you may not be able to continue following the optimal heading. You may have to move sideways, backtrack, or not move at all. The decision to stop and hide somewhere is a very difficult one. On the one hand, by stopping you would lose time and maybe reduce the distance between you and the opposition. On the other hand, you may not be able to keep up the pace. You may be exhausted or faced with dogs who can outrun you anyway. Depending on the situation, your strategy may call for a prolonged pause or for alternating a run with pauses in hiding. One thing to keep in mind, however, is that moving attracts more attention than remaining stationary. At some point, you may even come to the decision to stop and wait for nighttime.

A winning strategy, in this business as in most other situations, includes being able to tell when it is worth it to press on and when the game is up. Of course, the more desperate you are to get away, the more you will be willing to fight and take risks. If your capture means being killed, then you have nothing to lose and should fight to the end. In a bitter fight for survival, you will have to make a lot of quick decisions under enormous stress. You could be tired, in fear, and even sick. And yet you will need all of your strength, both physical and psychological.

As you continue on your march, you might be faced with the approach of ground forces and a helicopter hovering above. If one officer reaches you, you might decide to resist. But if you are facing two or more armed officers, you will not have much of a chance and giving up would be reasonable in all but the most extreme circumstances. The same can be said if an officer and his dog corner you. The dog can attack your feet and your hands while the officer draws his gun. If it's not a police officer but a criminal, then he will probably use his gun on you and your journey ends. There may also be cases of course where the police decide to take no prisoners, and that is something you need to determine based on the place where you are and the opposition you are facing.

If a trained police dog runs ahead of his handler following your scent or noise and catches up with you, you may still have a chance. As long as no person is with the dog, you can try and dispose of the animal. Using a firearm is out of the question as the noise, the smoke, and smell of the shot will give you away. You may be able to beat even a powerful dog with your bare hands but at great cost to you. These animals are trained to go for your feet or for your hands, especially if they see you are holding or about to grab something. If you are right-handed, you can grab something, like a stick or a bottle, with your left hand to distract the dog and let it go for it. While you push the object and your hand toward the dog's mouth, you quickly pull your knife with your right hand, stab him in the throat and rip. That should take care of things but, if not, you will face major problems. Once your stabbing attempt fails, the dog will be sure to go for the hand holding the knife, which he will surely get, or for your throat. Trying to kill a powerful dog with your bare hands is tough. An average size man can beat an average size dog but a German Shepard or Doberman will present a bigger challenge. Reports of men lifting up a large dog by the throat until the neck snaps are not very credible.

If you are successful in eliminating the dog threat, you will need to move quickly before the handler catches up with you. This time you will be moving steadily away from your pursuers for as long as you can. Keep on going toward your destination, and don't stop for anything. Mentally try to suppress pain, fatigue, and fear. Keep on going and you will be all right. Run, baby, run.

The escape model described above focuses on destinations reachable by car or public transportation. Travel to more distant locations, however, requires a different kind of planning. Even though we would never recommend regular airline travel, general aviation, as in private charters, can offer reasonable solutions.

If your final destination is in South America and you are traveling from Canada or the U.S., in theory you could go by land the entire way. As we have pointed out earlier, most borders on the journey south can be easy to cross without too many formalities, if any. There are, however, many borders, and the cumulative risk of all of those crossings can become significant. You may, therefore, consider chartering a small plane, such as a Cessna or Piper, to reach the South American mainland. Of course, the pilot should be a bush pilot who knows how to fly in and out of remote locations with dirt landing strips. She should also be familiar with under-the-radar flying. But, remember, you are only a passenger, and the fewer the questions, the better. Hear no evil, see no evil.

A typical starting point for an incognito flight into South America could be the southwest area of the Everglades in Florida. You can reach that area in many ways, including perhaps public transportation. You would then meet your pilot at the landing strip. Estimating an approximate distance of 1,300 nautical miles, you will typically need to fit the airplane with a ferry tank and at least 50 gallons of fuel. Additional necessary equipment will be wet suits and a self-inflatable raft. After takeoff, the plane should maintain a very low altitude, possible because of flat terrain and low vegetation in the Everglades. You would then proceed at low altitude over the Gulf of Mexico, and gradually rise to a cruising altitude as you leave U.S. airspace. You would then fly well west of Cuba, giving that country a wide berth. Then a direct shot south to the Guajira Peninsula of Colombia. The problem with the Florida-Colombia route is that it is used by narco-traffickers and, therefore, heavily patrolled by U.S. law enforcement, including monitoring by C-10 airplanes. An alternative route could be flying from the Texas coast and then over the Gulf of Mexico.

The Guajira peninsula of Colombia, which also covers a small part of Venezuela, has some flat, low, and desertic terrain that is ideal for low-altitude flying. The area also has quite a few dirt landing strips with which your pilot should be well acquainted. Most of the area is inhabited by local Indian tribes, a population known to be insular and not very interested in interaction with outsiders. Once you arrive in the peninsula, it is recommended that you head south and away from the area at your earliest convenience. An Anglo-looking person would stand out in the Guajira as a sore thumb. And, given the large drug traffic in the area, the general assumption is that a newly arrived gringo is either a wholesale buyer or a narc. And the life-span of narcs in the area is considerably shorter than elsewhere.

4. Settling Down

You have just arrived at your destination. If you have followed one of our suggestions, you may be walking into your very own little hut, away from the opposition, the cold (or heat), the danger, and the fear. You are home. Out with the old, in with the new. You have the panic bag with you and the basic necessities you have previously equipped the hut with. You go to the bedroom, lie down and sleep–a long and deep sleep–your first one in the Land of the Disappeared.

You wake up to a new reality, but it feels like a dream, so far away from the nightmare you left behind. At first you feel slightly confused, almost in shock. You are trying to process all that happened in the last few days. But then your usual energy returns, you feel blessed and look forward to a new day. The first order of business is to go shopping for groceries and other items you have not had time to bring to the house during preparations for the vanishing act. If you managed to get a bike in the hut, off you go pedaling into the sunny morning.

Eventually, you will need to retrieve your belongings from storage, if you have any, but not yet. That is a delicate task. If for some reason you were followed to the storage place when you were moving your belongings there, that location, now that you are safe, would be a major liability, connecting your old life with the new. And, depending on the amount of belongings you have left in storage, you would need a truck or at least a car to retrieve them. If the storage was known to the opposition, they would probably keep an eye on it. They may make arrangements with the renting office if it is a self-storage unit. They would be looking for anyone accessing the unit in the storage place, their car or truck, and the registration plate. That could lead the opposition to you and your new location. For those reasons, we recommend that you wait as long as possible to retrieve your belongings from storage. At the right time, you may want to send someone *not* connected with you to get your belongings and deliver them to a third location where you can safely go yourself.

Depending on many variables, you might eventually be able to buy a car. But even for limited use, we urge you not to. It is much better to stick as long as possible to bikes, electric bikes, mopeds, and other vehicles that do not require state licensing and plates.

Bike around town, walk, and take in the sights. Go to a couple of bars, and rehearse your legend. Start making new acquaintances and friends. Get to know your new environment. As you start on a routine, you will be getting used to the new surroundings. You will start running into the same people. You will get used to them, as they will get used to you. Eventually, the Land of the Disappeared will feel like home.

In addition to getting to know stores and services around you, you may want to see a doctor even if you are feeling well. Complain of something like the flu, so that you can start building a new history to solidify your legend. Just as you dismantled your old self, you now need to build a new one. You need to start generating the same kind of data you worked so hard to remove from databases. You can join a gym, get some store discount cards, or join clubs if there are any in your area.

Recreating a normal and contemporary persona might be necessary. You would have trouble even interacting with people if you lived totally off the grid. But you do not have to completely bury yourself in the digital world and the oppression it brings with it. Perhaps you have decided to run in order to get away from all that. If so, you can now seek a simpler life, the way things used to be before mobile phones and the Internet. And if your escape was only dictated by the needs of survival, you would still be well advised to limit activities that may bring you into contact with your past and the opposition.

At some point, you may need to start working, whether you have a financial need or not. It is healthy for you to really concentrate on work because it will help you anchor yourself in the Land of the Disappeared and, hopefully, even earn some money. Work relationships and networking are a fundamental part of connecting with society, which is why retired people who do not work even part time or volunteer often end up isolated and lonely. Employment, however, can be a very dangerous thing in the Land of the Disappeared. Except for the most menial of jobs, most employers in developed countries now require IDs. They also want to see a tax number and verify employment histories and references. Unless you have built a legend set in stone and backed by all manner of documents and references, we do not recommend that you apply for a job at this stage. For the legality of any documentation you wish to use, we encourage you to consult with an attorney in your new area.

As we said earlier, the best approach to a gainful occupation while safeguarding your privacy is self-employment. As part of your vanishing act preparations, you should have set up a corporate entity and generated business materials. This is the time to do all of the necessary printing of brochures and business cards if you have not done so already. You could then start promotion of your new business by mailing your materials or handing them personally to those individuals and businesses that may need your services. You could also hire a webmaster to help you put together a website for your business. Logos, tag lines, testimonials are all useful, but not your picture. And that is why social media, which can be useful to promote a business, is such a bad idea at this stage of your new life.

We have discussed earlier the modalities for acquiring new bank accounts, phones, and Internet tools such as email addresses. Through your new business, you can now implement some of those strategies. As soon as your activity starts, you will be well positioned to approach a bank and request to open a corporate account. A bank will have a favorable view of a new business; new income; and, most important, a new client. Opening a new account for the privacy minded, however, is tricky because of all of the new regulations on identity documents and other requirements. But at least, initially, you could use less formal payment tools such as PayPal or third parties.

Your new business may also require a domain name for the website, and that is often sold in a bundle with new email addresses that you can use. The company selling domain names, maybe through your webmaster, will be happy to create your new online profile as well. And that will also help you. But don't get carried away. Keep it simple, and always keep in mind that less is more.

At this point, if you weren't looking for privacy or on the run, you may be tempted to set up social media accounts, maybe the same as you had before. For the love of God, do not do it. For one thing, you would need to post pictures and that would be a huge mistake for all of the reasons we discussed in previous chapters. Also, sooner or later, you will trip. Even assuming new computers, phones, email addresses, and software, there is always the danger that, somehow, the new persona you carefully created will cross the old one. Details of the new may get cross referenced with the old. Of course, in modern society it is considered strange to not be on social media, and it may even arouse suspicion. When asked about it, perhaps you can say that you are "old fashioned," or just make up a story about a stalker or whatever.

Separated from family and old friends, sooner or later, you will need to get into a relationship, but not just yet. You need to get stronger in your sense of belonging. You need deeper roots and more local terms of reference. When the right person comes along, you will also need to make some important decisions. The biggest one will be whether to "kiss and tell" about your past. If you do, you would be creating a huge exposure for yourself. And if the relationship does not last, you will have created a permanent risk for nothing. If the relationship fails and turns into a bitter one, your partner may use your revelations against you. Is it then worth it to give up everything you built and start over? But if you do not come clean, then you may be living with guilt and in fear that, at some point, your history may come back to haunt you. And your partner may feel betrayed by your not telling them the truth and refuse to accept it. You would be getting no support. We do not have an answer for this type of dilemma as, in the end, these are very personal types of decisions.

Our general approach to personal relationships in the Land of the Disappeared is that you should keep your past to yourself for as long as possible. You can, however, tell your presumptive story in a way that it parallels biographical reality. The names and locations may be different, but many things remain the same. Moments of happiness and triumph, disappointments, and memories of family members and old loves can remain as long as you keep it a bit vague. One word of caution, however. Be careful about making up an adoption or saying that your parents died in a plane crash because such events can be verified through simple searches. Normally, one would not expect casual acquaintances to embark on a search of your past. But someone who plans to marry you may want to know a bit more than your tales about the pampas in Argentina or the Canadian prairies.

NINE

AUTHOR'S CHOICES

1. A Vacation Without End

This is a long-term plan but not a very difficult one. Imagine a lovely spot that you truly like but where you have never registered in a hotel or otherwise left official records of your visit. It could be a beach town; a mountain village; or one of those small, quaint towns where people retire. Ideally, it should be a somewhat transient location where both visitors and new residents go. You do not want an extremely provincial town where everybody knows everybody else, and an outsider would stand out like a sore thumb. Start going to this place with a certain frequency, always using your new identity, nickname, or whatever you have decided to use. Be careful, however, to never drive your car unless you park it at a great distance from the places you plan to visit. Make absolutely sure that you do not get a parking ticket. In all your conversations with locals, you should use the legend you have created for yourself that we discussed above, but make sure you are consistent with your story. Go shopping; go to restaurants, cafes, and bars. Talk to locals, and visit real estate agents to inquire about rentals and purchases. Always talk about your legend, your new you.

As you keep going to this place on vacation, you will find that people remember you and your legend. Make a point to stop and say hello wherever you have been before and met shopkeepers and others. Catch up on the latest local news and gossip. Learn who got married or died, the latest building developments, or a local scandal. Comment on this news, and remain polite but friendly. Talk about your "hometown," and make comparisons with local housing. Inquire about purchasing a bicycle, a canoe, or whatever makes sense in that location. Flirt with someone of the opposite sex, or your own if that is your orientation, but never go too far at this stage. Start discussing your plans of moving there. Ask for advice. Ask about different neighborhoods, communities, crime rates, and costs.

After many visits, you will become like a regular. And locals may actually start talking about you or even gossiping. But all these people will know and discuss is your legend. Unless you get into a serious conflict, no one will have a reason to research or investigate your background. You will be taken at face value.

When you are finally ready for your move, you can purchase a small home or apartment in this vacation place. You will have to pay cash, using the techniques explained in the section of this book on assets. A living trust may actually be the best vehicle to acquire the new property. But make absolutely sure that nothing in the trust documents can connect to your old identity. You may have to leave a copy of the trust document with the realtor or title company. You do not want any property or title search to link back to your old identity.

Once settled in, you can gradually start or continue changing your appearance. You can change your hair color, clothing, and other details that distinguished you until your move. In time, you will be home, among friends and loved ones.

2. Finding Peace in Conflict

In the world today, there are many areas that are experiencing conflict. Of course, that has always been the case; but in modern times, conflict is often followed by reconstruction and peace building with the participation and financing of a multitude of outsiders. Into that environment descend foreign armies, peacekeepers, national agencies, intergovernmental organizations, NGOs (nongovernmental organizations), private foundations, journalists, volunteers, people seeking work, adventurers, and smugglers and other types of criminals. The status and the length of stay of each person or organization can vary. The constant factor, however, is usually a non-functioning or fractured local government. Sometimes there are multiple governments controlling different parts of a country and separate authorities, military or civilian, having jurisdiction over a given area.

Because of the fractured or non-functioning authority, criminal activity thrives with people, drugs, and weapons being smuggled. ID documents end up being issued by various entities, often without coordination or consistent verification of biographical data. Entry and exit in conflict or post-conflict areas are either not controlled or regulated in different ways, depending on the specific area and the officials who man the border, if any. If there is a word that can describe all this, it is chaos. But chaos can bring opportunities for many who live on the fringes of society or wish to reinvent themselves, legally or not. And that could be you.

Generally speaking, natives of conflict or post-conflict regions have more important things to worry about than your biographical details or accreditation. In practice, if you are a foreigner in one of those areas, who is someone clearly not a member of the warring factions, you will enjoy special privileges and respect. Everyone will assume that you are there as part of some national or international contingent. And those organizations are essentially the ones that support the local economy. Locals often find employment as drivers, interpreters, movers, and in all of the support activities that the international community needs. As an "international," you will enjoy respect from the locals, including whatever police force they have, if any. If you state that you are there for a certain purpose, it is unlikely that you would be challenged. If you are someone looking for the ultimate anonymity and chose to do so in a conflict or post-conflict zone, however, some planning is needed.

Your plan to insert yourself and disappear in a conflict zone starts with the choice of an area. Some Google searches can give you a pretty good idea as to what to expect at any given time. Through another Internet search, you can then pick a catchy organization name that is not already taken. Once you have settled on an appropriate-sounding name, like "Peace Now," "Together in Peace," or other similar name, you can form a corporation or a nonprofit foundation. Or just skip formalities and use the name. If you are a detail-oriented person, you can even design a logo and copyright it to give more substance to your creation. You then create a basic website that lists your new persona as president and a variety of imaginary directors and advisors, whose email addresses you control. Business cards and brochures can easily be printed anywhere, but try to avoid your neighborhood printer. Always remember that printers and copying machines, in addition to computers, have long memories (that last until they are decommissioned and destroyed). Going a step further, you can create an ID card from your organization. It will have your name (your new incarnation that is), title, organization name and logo, and your signature somewhere prominent. If you are going to put an expiration date on it, try to give yourself some time. No point in printing something that expires next month, since you are the one issuing it anyway. You then laminate it and are good to go. Printing an ID card from your organization may not be illegal *per se*, but better check with your lawyer anyway. And chances are that in a conflict zone, they have no specific regulations on the design of organization IDs.

After you enter the conflict area with your new credentials, you find the office, or one of the offices, that issues accreditations. That should provide you with another, more formal ID or pass, which you can use for entering restricted areas and offices, and attending briefings or meetings. With time and a little luck, by working the pubs and other social venues, you might be able to get one of the people in charge of some authority or other to issue you yet another identity card, this time an official government one. And, some day, that may become a national passport of the new nation that emerges from the conflict. You will then have found your own peace in a place of conflict.

3. Creative Housing in the Land of the Disappeared

Let the Wind Carry You (or not)

One of the most interesting and pleasant environments one can find is that of a boating community. Boaters like to distinguish themselves as either power boaters or sailors and, indeed, some marinas, publications, boat shows, and advertising are geared to one boater type or the other. Most boaters, however, share the same passion for the water, an aptitude for problem solving, self-reliance, and a spirit of adventure.

Boats of a certain size can give the owner a certain degree of freedom. If you own a boat, you can live aboard; you can travel; and, on large sailboats, even cross oceans. That means immersing yourself in nature, going with the elements, and reaching any destination in the world without the usual shackles of government control. It can thus be said that, in this age of ubiquitous surveillance, sailing is the last frontier of freedom and the ultimate retreat for free spirits and adventurers who wish to be independent.

As a practical matter, however, a nomadic lifestyle on a boat is not for everyone. In addition to the necessity of sailing skills, there are numerous obstacles and challenges that such a lifestyle presents. Climate conditions and weather events, as well as mechanical issues that are normal occurrences elsewhere, can become life and death situations. The same is not true for boats that are more or less stationary and securely tied to a marina slip. Many people also live on dry-docked boats. Houseboats, whether in the water or "on the hard" (out of the water) are similar to a small house but have the advantage that they can be moved elsewhere, assuming they are operational or can be towed.

While all vessels are supposed to be registered somewhere, laws vary greatly from jurisdiction to jurisdiction. Unlike aircraft, the formalities to register a vessel used for pleasure (as opposed to commercial use) can be quite limited or even next to nil. You can title a vessel to a person, corporation, trust, foundation, and any other entities you can think of. And that is assuming you are going to register it at all, which some people do not do. Most of the earlier discussion on real estate can apply here, except that boats can move and, therefore, offer a plethora of jurisdictional choices; whereas the purchase and use of a parcel of land has to comply with local regulations.

When you are boating, you can encounter various kinds of authorities, from the coast guard to the navy and others. Incidentally, that is also true if you are staying in place at your slip or mooring. Unless they are transiting busy areas near maritime borders or where there are smuggling issues, however, boats are seldom stopped and even more rarely boarded. If you are trying to fly (or sail, that is) under the radar, you would, therefore, be well advised to stay away from areas known for drug trafficking or other criminal activities.

When entering or exiting a country, you are supposed to check in and out with the proper custom and immigration authorities at a designated point of entry. Our lawyers told us to mention this. That said, if you look at a map of the world, or any given country that is not landlocked, you will notice that for every official entry point, there are enormous stretches of unmanned coastline, some of them even private. For example, you could sail from Norway to a bay in the U.S. state of Maine, then onto a river, and finally to a creek and your house dock without exchanging a word with any humans. You could then tie up the boat, go to the bathroom, and take a shower. Who can say you ever left the house?

For those who are looking for a more permanent home, there are many marinas that allow liveaboards. Liveaboards make their boat a permanent or second home, and they are usually charged a little more than regular slip holders to cover electricity and other utilities. Marinas can be a friendly and very private environment if you pick the right one. Boaters tend to look after one another and share a bond that you would seldom find among landlubbers. There is often an unspoken code among people living in a marina that discourages too many personal questions. In that sense, a boating community has similarities with conflict areas mentioned above. Different situations but a common desire for privacy. Among liveaboards, you can find adventurers, drifters, creative people, free spirits, corporate dropouts, fugitives from justice and many other characters that, for one reason or another, prefer not to discuss too many details of their past. What better place is there to get away from it all than to move to a marina? But the trick is to find the right one.

In selecting a marina, you need to seriously consider its location. Anything too far from an urban area will force you to constantly rely on your car for your daily needs. You will need to drive to go shopping for food and other necessities. If the marina does not have a chandler, then you will need to travel to some other place or marina that does have a chandler to purchase various boat supplies. Excessive isolation is also not good for a variety of other reasons that in the end can increase the chances of exposure. A medical emergency, a fire, sinking, or other such event can be much harder to handle if you are away from urban areas. A marina in a densely populated city can offer a measure of anonymity but also excessive foot traffic and allow the opposition to infiltrate it and blend in better than it could in a more private location. Big-city marinas also tend to be expensive and seldom allow liveaboards, or they have long waiting lists. If you are a little bit in a hurry because you skipped the preparation stage of Plan B, then you might as well forget about a downtown marina.

An important distinction in the choice of marina is between informal boatyards with docks and other facilities, and more tidy places that cater to expensive yachts and wealthier people. The latter category should clearly be avoided because they usually do not allow liveaboards, do not permit boat owners to work on their boats, and have many other restrictions that make them unsuitable for your purposes. Even if you could get around all of the restrictions, someone looking for real privacy and anonymity would stand out and risk exposure. Fancy marinas will insist on seeing registration documents, insurance certificates, and may even run a credit check.

An exception to the general principles discussed above is that of river and canal boats. These can be found in many places in northern Europe such as the north of France, the UK, the Netherlands, Scandinavia, and other countries. Obviously, the larger the city and the more central you want to be, the more competition you will find for docking space. If you choose rural areas, you will have a plethora of choices and some even reasonably priced. There are even places where you can tie up for free, at least for a limited amount of time. But even in the center of some cities, and we omit details here to protect the innocent, you can find situations where a space can be had for next to nothing, either legally, or with the tolerance of the authorities. Even in the midst of a housing crisis where apartments are hard to find or are outrageously expensive, you may be able to find a place for your boat with great views of the water and historic landmarks.

In terms of geographic location, as in other situations we have previously discussed, we do not recommend places with extreme weather. A very cold place creates many complications such as heating the boat, which can be expensive since most boats are not too well insulated. When the water freezes, many more needs arise to keep the boat safe. Ice on the ground or on the boat can also present significant challenges and can greatly increase the chances of your slipping and getting injured. That would be bad in any circumstance but particularly if you are trying to lay low. An area prone to hurricanes can also be a bad idea for a permanent mooring.

It's never fun when a hurricane hits. But if a boat represents your home, your investment, your safety, and your only chance at anonymity, a direct hit could be catastrophic even if you physically survive it. And even without a direct hit, a serious storm will usually be followed by a surge. If you are not on the boat and checking on her, as the water rises, the lines can tighten and eventually break. That can result in either a sinking or in the boat breaking free of her mooring, both disastrous outcomes. The best approach is, therefore, to find a marina in a quiet area in a temperate zone.

Before you settle down in a marina or on a canal, you need to secure ownership or rental of a boat. Rental is a straightforward process, except for the paperwork and background verification that that might entail. Boat rental is also quite rare, and you can't expect to find it in the marina or canal you select. Ownership and registration, as we discussed above, can be accomplished in different ways. The problem with buying a boat and taking it to the marina you select, however, is that you will be forced to do many things that are not prudent if you are trying to lay low. First off, the boat needs to be seaworthy or be made to be. Then she will have to be registered somewhere and probably insured, which may require a survey. Then she has to be sailed or towed to the marina, and there you will face additional paperwork and controls. Shipping it by truck is a possibility, but the cost would be high and the paperwork significant. The best approach, in our opinion, is to buy an old boat that is *already* in the marina where you want to be. If you purchase her in cash, which you should do anyway, you will just take over the slip or storage contract and relax. The seller will be happy to get cash, will sign title, and will be out of the picture. The marina will also be happy if you give a substantial down payment. Your intention will be of course to register the boat in "your own" name or company, but you can bet no one will remember to check on these minor details in an informal, laid-back marina. Your boat neighbors might not even notice the change in ownership, as the boat will stay where she is until you are ready to sail, if you ever are. Sooner or later, you will be tempted to rename the boat. But you should avoid catchy names like "Ms. Behaving," "Double Trouble," "Ms. Chief," or "Criminal Intent." Funny, maybe, but do you really want to call attention to your newfound hobby and home?

Land Yachts

As we have seen, a life on the water carries with it the promise of unlimited freedom and adventure. A world without bounds and borders. A life lived close to nature and away from the complications and rules of modern society. That is only in theory, however, as many regulations do affect boaters. In order to sail, you also need a properly equipped vessel and skills. You need to be in pretty good shape. You are subject to the vagaries of the weather and seasons. If you sail offshore, you may be facing long periods of isolation. Illness or injury aboard can become life threatening. A windy night at anchor can easily become a sleepless night.

A more practical option for a life on the move is that of an RV. RVs, which stand for recreational vehicles, include travel trailers, motorhomes, camper vans, and truck campers. Those vehicles are not to be confused with mobile homes that are cheap, stationary houses that are only moved twice: to the home site first and soon afterwards to the dumpster. The difference between the RV lifestyle and living on a boat is that, for all intents and purposes, an RV can give you much more freedom. You can move whenever you want without regard to ordinary weather conditions. And if you make the right choices, you can get most of the comforts of home while on the road–or on the run!

RVs used to have a bad image, especially those that are permanently parked. They were thought to be used by homeless people or drifters. In some countries, they were the hallmark of gypsies. Much has changed in the last few years. During the COVID pandemic, many people became uncomfortable living in crowded cities. Staying in hotels when traveling was considered dangerous. Remote work became common and remains common to this day. In many cases, it is now possible to work while on the move. You can combine a tedious desk job with travel and adventure. Many publications such as *Van Life* and others cater to a younger, better educated group of people that tend to have some disposable income. Even YouTube now features many videos of traveling couples, families, and single people. All of that has created a growing community of people on the move that includes educated young adults working in advertising; or as journalists, photographers, bloggers, and influencers. Others with limited means are just out for adventure on a budget.

As mentioned above, RVs come in different types. Travel trailers are those vehicles that are towed by an SUV or pickup truck and have no motor. They are cheaper than motorized vehicles and use all the interior space for accommodations, which can make them quite comfortable. They are a good choice for someone who needs temporary housing while only occasionally moving. They are also a good choice for a family traveling on a budget. But they are very limited, as they can't go anywhere without a towing vehicle. And the towing itself can present its own complications, not to mention the parking limitations, both practical and legal. For example, in most cities, you cannot park trailers overnight, and that is also true of some residential subdivisions.

At the other extreme, camper vans have much more limited accommodations, and most of them are downright cramped for more than one occupant. But they are self-propelled and can go anywhere, almost like a regular SUV. Motor homes are somewhat in between. They are also self-propelled but have better accommodations than a van. Depending on size, they can be more difficult to drive and park. Another option is the truck camper, which consists of a self-contained camper mounted on a large pickup truck. In theory, the superstructure can be removed and left where desired. That creates the option of parking the camper and using the truck for general driving, but the time and hassles involved in removing the superstructure to free the truck can be considerable. A benefit of that arrangement, however, is that one can choose the camper but also the engine of the truck that is bought separately. You don't have that choice with a motorhome or van. In all cases, we would recommend a diesel engine, not only for efficiency and power but also for range.

The choice of RV is dictated by the specific needs of the person or family. For privacy seekers on the move and those in need of getting away in a hurry, we would recommend camper vans or very small motorhomes. Truck campers are also a good choice with the added benefit that, unlike all other vehicles, the superstructure in most jurisdictions does not need to be registered and does not need license plates. If you park the superstructure alone somewhere unattended, it would not give away any personal information such as a license plate would. One possible drawback of truck campers for people in precarious circumstances is that the cab of the pickup is not connected to the camper. That means that if you are relaxing in the camper and suddenly realize you need to depart in a hurry, you will need to exit the camper, and then enter the cab of the pickup, thereby possibly exposing yourself to hostiles.

In spite of the clear differences among the various types of RVs, the decision on which vehicle to purchase is a complex one. On the one hand, any large rig, especially a trailer, is going to limit parking and other options. It is also going to make a quick exit much more complicated than would be the case in a van. But the final destination and the intended length of stay are also crucial factors. What might be acceptable for a couple of days may be intolerable for the long haul. You, therefore, need to ask yourself not only what the basic minimum for survival is but also what would make you happy. Just because you find yourself in pressing circumstances or are, God forbid, a fugitive, it does not mean you should give up all comforts. Nice music, a film, or a good book in a warm cozy place can relax you and improve your mood. And you may need to be in the best of moods when the opposition comes knocking.

TEN

THE HUMAN FACTOR

———

This is the final chapter of this book. Here's hoping that you have enjoyed the read so far and that it has sparked some exciting new ideas, or at least entertained you. All good things, however, must come to an end. So here we are with a reality check–a dose of reality not meant to cast doubt on the many escape strategies in the book, but a focus on the weakest link of all: *you*!

If you are serious about taking back your privacy and moving on to a quieter or different existence, you need some introspection to understand the reasons behind your desire for an exit. Easy enough if you are in fear of your life or, God forbid, running from the law. But if, deep down, you are just looking for love, this Plan B may not be for you. If what you are looking for are more human connections than you have already accumulated, we cannot help you. At the core of this book is the power of silence and withdrawal. Any new existence calls for a strategy to gradually dismantle and empty your current life. And we are not just talking about taking down Facebook.

Signing off from a life of engagement requires purpose and determination. It requires being happy with yourself without the constant support of a noisy world around you. You need to rediscover your inner self, the child in you, just as it was many years ago before you lost your innocence.

After you have disengaged from whatever you are running from, you need not expect a life of solitude without emotional support. There can be a full life and joy in the Land of the Disappeared. But if you do it right, it will never be the same as it once was. You will have regained a measure of yourself that you can never share with others, your own little world where no one can go.

Wishing you happy and safe travels, we hope you can find your way home.

The End

ABOUT THE AUTHOR

GD Applegate is an international lawyer, investigator, traveler, and adventurer. The author of several books and articles, Applegate has become increasingly concerned about the growing reach of online companies and the resulting invasion of people's privacy. Extensive travel, ranging from places of idyllic beauty to conflict zones, combined with professional experience and research, have made this book possible. The author's goal is to offer readers some strategies to make their private life more *private*. Or, at least, to entertain them while they dream of their own Plan B.